Contents

Using this thesaurus 4

Reading this thesaurus 5

Parts of speech 6

The thesaurus 8

Topic words 122

Adventures, Animals, Buildings,
Clothes, Colours, Cooking, Feelings,
Groups, Human body, Materials,
Movement, Music, Taste, Weather

Overused words 125

bad, get, go, have, lovely, move,
nice, put, say, take, very

Using this thesaurus

This thesaurus will help you to:

• find alternatives to a word so you do not keep repeating it.

• make your writing more interesting and varied.

• help you to say exactly what you mean.

How to find a word in this thesaurus:

• Choose a word that you want to find an alternative for.

• The words are arranged in alphabetical order. Look at the first letter of the word. Go to the section of the thesaurus that covers that letter. Use the alphabet down the side of each page to help you find the right section.

• The words above the coloured line at the top of each set of two pages show you the first and last words on those pages.

• If you cannot find your word, check that you have spelt it correctly. Remember to take off word endings, such as 'ing' and 'ed', before looking for the word. If you still cannot find it, check at the back of the book, starting on page 122, where some common words are listed. If it is not there either, you will need to look in a bigger thesaurus.

The same but different?

Some of the words listed in the thesaurus are synonyms (say *sin-o-nims*). They mean the same as the original word. **Big** means the same as **large**. These two words are synonyms.

Some of the words listed are similar to the original word, but a little bit different in meaning. The words **cross** and **furious** are similar, but **furious** really means 'very cross'.

Reading this thesaurus

All the words on the page start with this letter.

This shows the first word on the page.

These letters explain which part of speech a word is. It could be a noun (n), a verb (v) or an adjective (adj). See page 6 to find out more about parts of speech.

This shows the last word on the page.

Here you can find the opposite of the word.

Some words have more than one meaning. Each number gives a different meaning.

This sentence gives an example of how the word might be used.

Parts of speech

Noun (n)

A noun is a naming word.
You know a word is a noun if you you can put the word 'the' or 'a' in front of it. Some nouns are things you can touch:

door

glove

school

tree

Some nouns are things you cannot touch:

language

trouble

sound

week

Proper noun

A proper noun is the name of a specific person or place. It begins with a capital letter:

Anna

Australia

Tony

London

Adjective (adj)

An adjective describes a noun:

big

soft

happy

pretty

tall

old

shiny

spooky

Verb (v)

A verb is a doing or being word:

act

drink

look

talk

jump

write

swim

read

Most verbs have these endings:

walk: walk**s**, walk**ing**, walk**ed**

dance: dance**s**, danc**ing**, danc**ed**

jump: jump**s**, jump**ing**, jump**ed**

Adverb

An adverb describes a verb. Most adverbs end in 'ly':

quick**ly**

nice**ly**

smooth**ly**

tight**ly**

But some adverbs do not end in 'ly':

soon

enough

upstairs

again

Connective words

These words are sometimes called conjunctions. You use them to join two sentences together:

and

but

because

so

a
b
c
d
e
f
g
h
i
j
k
l
m
n
o
p
q
r
s
t
u
v
w
x
y
z

Aa

about

1. roughly, approximately, around, more or less, close to
I ran **about** 400 metres.

2. on, relating to, dealing with, concerning
She read a book **about** cats.

above

1. over, higher than
The plates are on the shelf **above** the bowls.

2. more than, higher than, better than
My mark was **above** average.
opposite: *below*

abroad

overseas, another country
They went **abroad** for their holiday.

accident (n)

crash, pile-up, smash, collision
He was hurt in a traffic **accident**.

accident

accidentally, by mistake, unintentionally
She dropped the laptop **by accident**.
opposite: *on purpose, deliberately*

act (n)

1. deed, action, thing to do
Helping the lost dog was a kind **act**.

2. pretence
He's not really mean – it's just an **act**.

activity (n)

pastime, hobby, thing to do
My favourite **activity** is climbing.

actually

1. genuinely, truly, really, completely
I can't believe it's **actually** dark already.

2. in fact
Actually, I've decided to stay at home today.

admit (v)

1. confess, own up, reveal, acknowledge
Nancy had to **admit** that she hadn't done her homework.

2. allow in
No one will be **admitted** before seven o'clock.

adult (n)

grown-up
Children have to go with an **adult**.

adventure (n)

exploit, exciting experience, expedition
The sailor told them about his **adventure**.
See also page 122

afraid (adj)

frightened, scared, terrified, worried (by), anxious (about)
I am **afraid** of large spiders.

again

1. once more, another time
Olivia loved the book so much that she read it **again**.

2. repeatedly, over and over
Joseph jumped **again** and **again**.

aid (n)

1. help, assistance
Grace gave **aid** to the stranded boy.

2. emergency help, relief, supplies
They sent **aid** to the earthquake zone.

aim (n)

goal, target, objective
The **aim** of this lesson is to learn about animals.

air (n)

1. sky
The bird flew through the **air**.

2. gas
The balloon was full of **air**.

3. atmosphere
The smoke spread through the **air**.

alarm (v)

startle, frighten, surprise, scare, shock, make jump
Loud noises **alarm** the dog.

alive (adj)

1. living, breathing, surviving
The cat was still **alive** after the accident.
opposite: *dead*

2. in existence, around
Sharks have been **alive** for millions of years.

all

every one, each
All of the children sang.
opposite: *none*

a
b
c
d
e
f
g
h
i
j
k
l
m
n
o
p
q
r
s
t
u
v
w
x
y
z

all right (adj)

1. unhurt, fine, OK, well, uninjured, unharmed
Luckily, she was **all right** after her bicycle broke.
2. not bad, OK, acceptable, adequate, satisfactory
Ben's story is **all right**, but Caitlin's is better.
3. allowed, permitted
It's **all right** to cycle on this path.

almost

nearly, not quite, approaching, close to
Sofia is **almost** eight years old.

alone (adj)

by oneself, solitary, isolated, unaccompanied
Alexander is **alone** on the island.

also

as well as, in addition to, besides, too, plus
Isabelle likes bananas and **also** strawberries.

alter (v)

change, adapt, adjust
We can **alter** the way we do that.

always

1. all the time, each time
Granddad **always** has a sleep after dinner.
opposite: *never*
2. forever
I will **always** love singing.

amazing (adj)

brilliant, wonderful, fantastic, incredible
She baked an **amazing** cake for his birthday.

amount (n)

quantity, sum
He had saved a large **amount** of money to buy a pet.

angry (adj)

cross, annoyed, furious, mad, irritated
Dad was **angry** because my ball smashed the window.

animal (n)

beast, creature
A large **animal** ran out of the forest.
See also page 122

answer (n)

reply, response, solution
I didn't know the **answer** to the
teacher's question.

answer (v)

respond to, reply to
He had to **answer** the policeman's
questions even though he was tired.

appear (v)

turn up, arrive, materialize, show up
When the clock strikes midnight, the
ghost will **appear**.

approach (v)

go near, go close to, go towards
You shouldn't **approach** the
dangerous dog.

appropriate (adj)

suitable, ideal, expected, normal
Ice cream is not an **appropriate**
food for breakfast.

approximately

about, roughly, near enough, in the
region of, around
It is **approximately** 250,000 miles
to the moon.
opposite: *exactly*

area (n)

region, space, location, part, section
This **area** is reserved for competitors.

argue (v)

fight, squabble, bicker, quarrel
Please don't **argue** about who should
go first.

argument (n)

quarrel, squabble, row, dispute,
fight, disagreement
The girls had an **argument** about
whose turn it was.

arrange (v)

1. organize, sort out, plan
Alice says she will **arrange** the party
for the weekend.
2. set out, display
You should **arrange** the flowers in
a blue vase.

a b c d e f g h i j k l m n o p q r s t u v w x y z

a
b
c
d
e
f
g
h
i
j
k
l
m
n
o
p
q
r
s
t
u
v
w
x
y
z

arrive (v)

turn up, show up, come
Hassan will **arrive** in a helicopter.

ask (v)

1. query, enquire, find out
Yasmin went to **ask** when the film would start.

2. request
Please **ask** Jack to pick up the rubbish.

asleep (adj)

sleeping, snoozing, slumbering, dozing, napping
The cat was **asleep** by the fire.
opposite: *awake*

assistant (n)

helper
The magician pretended to saw his **assistant** in half!

astonished (adj)

amazed, astounded, surprised, shocked
James was **astonished** that the monster was still alive.

attach (v)

join, connect, link, fasten
Holly **attached** the chain to the bike.

attack (v)

assault, jump on, savage
The lion tried to **attack** his trainer.

attractive (adj)

good-looking, desirable, pretty, handsome
That is a very **attractive** house.

avoid (v)

1. shun, dodge, stay away from, steer clear of, give a wide berth to
I try to **avoid** my bossy uncle.

2. escape, get out of, skive
Ellie wanted to **avoid** her chores.

awful (adj)

horrible, horrid, disgusting, vile, nasty, dire, rank, foul, hideous
That lumpy custard is **awful**.

awkward (adj)

1. difficult, tricky, hard, inconvenient
It was **awkward** steering the boat round the tight corner.

2. embarrassed, uncomfortable
Lucas felt **awkward** explaining how he had broken the window.

Bb

baby (n)

infant, newborn, babe, tot
The **baby** lay in
a cradle.

back (n)

end, rear, tail-end
I was at the **back** of the queue.
opposite: *front*

back (v)

1. reverse, go backwards
I saw the car **back** into a post.

2. support
The teacher will **back** the children's
demand for a longer playtime.

back (adj)

hind, rear
The bear stood on its **back** legs.

bad (adj)

See page 125

ball (n)

sphere, round shape
Max squashed the clay into a **ball**.

ban (v)

prohibit, not allow, make illegal,
outlaw, forbid
They will **ban** phones from
the classroom.

bang (v)

bash, knock
The boy **banged** the
drum loudly.

bar (n)

1. rod, pole
There are **bars** across the window.

2. block, slab
Noah ate a whole **bar** of chocolate.

bar (v)

banish, throw out, exclude, ban,
kick out
They will **bar** dogs from the park.

barely

hardly, only just
The foal was **barely** able to stand.

bargain (n)

good deal, excellent price,
cheap item
Their flight was a **bargain**.

bark (v)

woof, yap, yelp, howl, growl, snarl
We heard the dog **bark**.

base (n)

bottom, foot
The climbers waited at the **base** of the mountain.
opposite: *top*

bash (v)

knock, hit, bump, crash
Lily **bashed** into the table.

be (v)

1. exist, live
Dylan would give anything to **be** somewhere else.

2. become, work as
Rosie wants to **be** an actor.

3. feel, behave
Don't **be** scared – I'll look after you.

beach (n)

coast, seaside
Leo loves to make sandcastles at the **beach**.

beast (n)

creature, monster, animal
The **beast** tried to attack the elf, but he ran away.

beat (v)

1. defeat, thrash, win against
We will **beat** the red team.

2. hit, strike, thrash, wallop
The evil wizard **beat** his apprentice.

beautiful (adj)

attractive, good-looking, handsome, pretty, lovely, gorgeous, stunning
What a **beautiful** puppy!

begin (v)

start, commence, get going
You can **begin** to eat your dinner now.

beginning (n)

start, launch, opening
Read it again from the **beginning**.
opposite: *ending*

believe (v)

1. accept, comprehend, conceive
I cannot **believe** that we lost.

2. think exist
Jake doesn't **believe in** ghosts.

below

1. under, beneath
There is a river running **below** the house.
2. less than, lower than
My score was **below** average.
opposite: *above*

bend (n)

curve, corner, kink, turn, twist, angle
There was a **bend** in the road.

bendy (adj)

supple, flexible, springy
A young tree has a **bendy** trunk.
opposite: *stiff*

bent (adj)

twisted, crooked, arched, hunched,
bowed, humped
The old man had a **bent** back.
opposite: *straight*

best (adj)

finest, preferred, top, supreme
Kathy baked the **best** apple tart.
opposite: *worst*

better (adj)

1. higher quality, superior (to),
preferable (to)
The green sweets are **better** than the
red ones.
opposite: *inferior (to)*

2. improve, enhance
You can make the cake **better**
by adding some more icing.

3. recover, get well, make progress,
improve, be healthier
You will **get better** if you take
the medicine.

big (adj)

large, huge, enormous, gaping, wide,
long, sizeable, massive, vast
There is a **big** hole in my coat.
opposite: *small*

bit (n)

piece, chunk, portion, fragment,
share, slice, lump
Can I have a **bit** of pie, please?

blame (v)

accuse, hold responsible, scold,
tell off
Don't **blame** me – I didn't do it!

a
b
c
d
e
f
g
h
i
j
k
l
m
n
o
p
q
r
s
t
u
v
w
x
y
z

blend (v)
mix, combine, stir together
Blend the blue and yellow to make green.

blot (n)
stain, mark, splodge, smudge, smear
There is a **blot** on the page.

blow up (v)
1. inflate, put air into
I need to **blow up** the balloons.

2. bomb
The soldiers are going to **blow up** a bunker.

blurred (adj)
fuzzy, out of focus, hazy, vague, blurry
The photo is **blurred** so I cannot see his face clearly.
opposite: *clear*

body (n)
1. figure, physique
The athlete has a well-toned **body**.

2. corpse, remains, carcass
They buried the hamster's **body** in the garden.

bog (n)
marsh, swamp, fen, quagmire
The giant lost his shoes in a **bog**.

bold (adj)
brave, confident, heroic, fearless, plucky, courageous
The **bold** knight attacked the dragon.

boring (adj)
dreary, dull, uninteresting
The film was so **boring** that I fell asleep.

bossy (adj)
overbearing, domineering, pushy
The **bossy** boy told his brother what to do.

bottom (n)

1. base, foot, lowest part
The hut is at the **bottom** of the hill.
opposite: *top*, *summit*

2. buttocks, rear, backside, rear end, bum, behind
He fell on his **bottom**.

bound (v)

leap, jump, spring, run, bounce
We watched a deer **bound** through the woods.

box (n)

case, crate, container, chest, packet, carton
The tomatoes are in a large **box**.

boy (n)

lad, young man, youth
There was a **boy** in a red shirt.

brainy (adj)

bright, intelligent, smart, clever
Ethan's **brainy** sister got full marks in her test.

brand (n)

make, type, label, design
Which **brand** of trainers do you like?

brave (adj)

courageous, heroic, unafraid, fearless, bold, daring, gutsy
The **brave** fireman went into the burning building.
opposite: *cowardly*

break (n)

1. gap, hole, crack, space
There is a **break** in the track.

2. rest, pause, interval, respite
Take a **break** and relax.

break (v)

snap, crack, split, fracture, divide, shatter
The ice will **break** if you walk on it.

breed (n)

type, variety, species, sort, kind
This **breed** of dog grows very large.

bright (adj)

1. brilliant, shining, blazing, dazzling, blinding, glaring
I was dazzled by the **bright** light.
opposite: *dim*

2. happy, cheerful, sunny, cheery
Toby's **bright** smile cheered me up.

3. clever, intelligent, brainy, smart, gifted, talented
Andrew is very **bright** and knows everything.

a
b
c
d
e
f
g
h
i
j
k
l
m
n
o
p
q
r
s
t
u
v
w
x
y
z

a
b
c
d
e
f
g
h
i
j
k
l
m
n
o
p
q
r
s
t
u
v
w
x
y
z

brilliant (adj)

1. excellent, exceptional, great, fantastic, outstanding, superb
I loved that book – it was **brilliant**!

2. bright, dazzling, blazing, shining brightly
A **brilliant** comet shot across the sky.

bring (v)

1. carry, deliver, transport
Bring the shopping into the kitchen.

2. raise, rear, care for, parent, look after
Parents should **bring up** their children properly.

broken (adj)

1. not working, destroyed, damaged, smashed, faulty
The toy is **broken** and cannot be fixed.
opposite: *intact, fixed*

2. fractured
My arm is **broken** – it really hurts!

bug (n)

1. insect, creepy-crawly, minibeast
We went into the garden to collect **bugs**.

2. infection, illness, disease
Stan has a stomach **bug**.

bug (v)

pester, nag, hassle, annoy, irritate
Don't **bug** me – let me read my book!

build (v)

construct, make, put together, put up
The boys decide to **build** an igloo from blocks of snow.

bully (v)

torment, push around, hassle, pick on
It is not right to **bully** people.

bump (n)

1. knock, swelling, lump
Kate has a nasty **bump** on her head.

2. lump, flaw, raised part, bulge
There is a **bump** in the paint.

bump (v)

hit, collide (with), crash (into), run (into), knock (against)
Dad will **bump into** something if he drives like that.

bumpy (adj)

1. irregular, uneven, lumpy
The glass won't stand up because the surface is **bumpy**.
opposite: *even*

2. uneven, jolting, bouncy, jerky
I felt sick from the **bumpy** ride.
opposite: *smooth*

bunch (n)

1. collection, group, cluster, set
Where is my **bunch** of keys?

2. bouquet, posy
Here is a **bunch** of flowers.

3. set, group, gang, crowd
I have a good **bunch** of friends.

burn (v)

1. scorch, singe, overcook, set fire to, scald, char
Archie will **burn** his finger if he touches the hot pan.

2. blaze, combust
A match **burns** very quickly.

busy (adj)

1. occupied, overworked, employed
My mum is too **busy** to take me shopping.

2. crowded, bustling, hectic, teeming
The shops are **busy** at Christmas time.

buy (v)

purchase, pay for
We went to **buy** fruit from the supermarket.
opposite: *sell*

a
b
c
d
e
f
g
h
i
j
k
l
m
n
o
p
q
r
s
t
u
v
w
x
y
z

a
b
c
d
e
f
g
h
i
j
k
l
m
n
o
p
q
r
s
t
u
v
w
x
y
z

Cc

café (n)

tea shop, coffee shop, restaurant, tearoom, snack bar, bistro
Hannah went to a **café** for tea.

call (v)

1. shout, call out, speak loudly, yell, exclaim
I heard Mum **call** from the garden.

2. phone, get in touch, ring, telephone
Grandpa will **call** you later.

3. drop by, visit, stop by, drop in, come round
Dad's friend will **call by** with an extra spanner.

calm (adj)

quiet, tranquil, even
The sea is very **calm** today.
opposite: *rough*

can (v)

is able to, is capable of
Eva **can** jump high, so she always wins at sports day.

care (n)

attention, help, aid
Grandma had the best **care** at the hospital.

care (v)

1. look after, nurture, attend to
Millie will **care for** her new kitten.

2. (be) concerned about, mind, (be) bothered about
Freya doesn't **care** if her face is clean or dirty.

career (n)

job, profession, occupation, work
What do you want to do for your **career**?

careful (adj)

gentle, cautious, attentive
Be **careful** when you carry the vase.
opposite: *careless*

carry (v)

1. transport, convey, transfer, lift
Tom had to **carry** the bag on his back.

2. continue, keep going with, persist in
I'll **carry on** asking till you agree!

3. perform, do, complete, accomplish
Carry out your tasks quickly.

case (n)
box, chest, trunk, suitcase, crate, bag, briefcase, luggage
All my books are in the **case**.

catch (v)
hold, seize, grab, stop, trap, capture
Erin tried to **catch** the runaway horse.

celebration (n)
festival, festivity, carnival, party
We had a lovely birthday **celebration**.

centre (n)
middle, midpoint, midst
There is a hole in the **centre** of my doughnut.

certain (adj)
sure, definite, confident, positive
I'm **certain** my brother is going to pass his spelling test.

chance (n)
1. risk, possibility, likelihood
There's a **chance** the ice will break.

2. opportunity
You won't have another **chance** to join the trip.

3. luck
Snap is a game of **chance**.

change (v)
1. swap, exchange
Mum went to the shop to **change** my dress for a bigger size.

2. alter, differ
The situation will never **change**.

3. adapt, adjust, alter, amend
Change the end of your story.

charge (v)
rush, storm, hurtle, run
Don't **charge** in here like that!

chase (v)
pursue, go after, follow, hunt
The lion will **chase** you if you get out of the car.

chat (n)
talk, conversation, natter, gossip
Freddie liked to have a **chat** with his friends instead of listening to the teacher.

a
b
c
d
e
f
g
h
i
j
k
l
m
n
o
p
q
r
s
t
u
v
w
x
y
z

cheap (adj)

reasonably priced, inexpensive
I have to buy that hat – it's
so **cheap**!

cheat (v)

1. act unfairly, fiddle
The boy **cheated** in the test.

2. con, swindle, trick, dupe
She **cheated** me out of my prize.

cheerful (adj)

happy, content, cheery, joyful, merry
The children are **cheerful** when
they play.
opposite: *grumpy*

chest (n)

1. trunk, case, crate
The pirate kept his treasure
in a **chest**.

2. breast
I'm going to the doctor's because
I have a pain in my **chest**.

chew (v)

bite, gnaw, chomp, nibble
The puppy likes to **chew** the rug.

child (n)

kid, youngster
Alex must go to school because he is
a **child**.

choice (n)

1. pick, selection
The shop has a huge **choice** of cakes.

2. option, possibility, alternative
There are three **choices**.

choose (v)

pick, select, decide
You can **choose** whether you go
swimming or sailing.

chop (v)

1. cut, dice, slice
Chop the carrots to make soup.

2. amputate, lop off, cut off
The surgeon **chopped off** the man's leg.

3. cut down, hack, slash, slice,
fell, saw
We must **chop down** the trees to
clear a space.

chunk (n)

lump, slab, bit, piece, portion
A **chunk** fell off the rock.

clap (v)
applaud, cheer
We will **clap** at the end of the play.

clean (v)
wash, scrub, clear, mop, sweep, polish, vacuum, hoover
Simon will **clean** the floor today.

clean (adj)
1. fresh, spotless, unmarked, washed
Put on a **clean** shirt to go to school.
opposite: *dirty*

2. pure, fresh, sterile, unpolluted
Drink only **clean** water or you may be ill.

clear (v)
tidy, move, get rid of, remove, pick up, put away
Please **clear** that mess off the floor.

clear (adj)
1. clean, transparent, pure, see-through
The water in the river is so **clear** you can see the fish.

2. obvious, plain
Make it **clear** what you want.

3. empty, open, free
There is a **clear** space around the campfire.

clever (adj)
smart, intelligent, bright, brainy, gifted, talented
Ben is **clever** – he is top of his class.

climb (v)
1. clamber up, scale, go up
Goats can **climb** steep mountains.

close (v)
shut, slam, pull to, lock, fasten
Close the door when you go out.

close
near, beside, adjoining, next to
My house is so **close** to the sea we can hear the waves.

closed (adj)
shut, not open, locked
The shop was **closed** on Sunday.
opposite: *open*

coat (n)
jacket, anorak, overcoat, raincoat, mac, cagoule, blazer
Put on a **coat** – it's cold!

a
b
c
d
e
f
g
h
i
j
k
l
m
n
o
p
q
r
s
t
u
v
w
x
y
z

cold (adj)

1. chilly, frosty, freezing, frozen, snowy, icy, wintry, nippy, bitter, raw
It's **cold** outside.
opposite: *warm*

2. unfriendly, severe, stern, hostile, stony
The king gave the beggar a **cold** look.
opposite: *friendly*

collect (v)

1. gather, pick up
Let's **collect** acorns.

2. fetch, bring, pick up
Izzy **collected** her brother from school.

colour (n)

hue, tone, shade
What **colour** sweet do you want?
See also page 122

colourful (adj)

bright, vibrant, multicoloured
They bought **colourful** scarves.

come (v)

1. arrive, get, turn up, return, show up
Mum will **come** home at six.

2. happen, occur, result, take place
Adam plans to join the army, **come** what may.

3. find, meet, bump into, discover, happen upon, encounter, come upon
You will **come across** three trolls by the river.

4. enter, walk in
Open the door and **come in**!

comfortable (adj)

snug, comfy, soft, easy, relaxing, warm, cosy
That armchair is very **comfortable**.

common (adj)

usual, ordinary, normal, widespread, frequently found, standard, everyday
Sparrows are very **common**.

complain (v)

grumble, moan, fuss, whinge, whine, carp, protest, nag, object (to)
Hassan **complained** about the bad food.

complete (adj)

whole, entire, finished
Poppy wants to collect the **complete** set of dolls.

confused (adj)

puzzled, mixed up, baffled, bewildered
She was too **confused** to answer.

cook (v)

prepare, heat up, roast, boil, fry, grill
Shall I **cook** the dinner now?
See also page 123

crack (n)

1. break, gap, split, chip
There is a **crack** in the pavement.

2. shot, boom, bang, snap, blast, pop
There was a loud **crack** of gunfire.

crack (v)

break, split, smash, splinter, shatter
You need to **crack** the coconut on a rock.

crash (n)

1. boom, crack, blast, smash, thunderclap
There was a loud **crash** as the building fell down.

2. pile-up, accident, smash
He was hurt in a car **crash**.

crawl (v)

creep, clamber, wriggle, slither, slide, writhe
The beetle **crawled** under the door.

crazy (adj)

mad, odd, deranged, nutty, wacky, bizarre
Be careful of the wizard – he's **crazy**.

create (v)

make, design, produce, build, form, invent, construct
We will **create** a model of our school.

creep (v)

sneak, sidle, edge, crawl, slink, tiptoe
Creep round the corner and go 'Boo!'

creepy (adj)

spooky, eerie, frightening, scary
The movie is too **creepy** to watch.

cross (adj)

annoyed, angry, furious, grumpy, bad-tempered, irritated
My teacher gets **cross** when I make a noise in class.

crowded (adj)

full, bustling, packed, teeming
I walked shyly into the **crowded** room.

cruel (adj)
spiteful, mean, unkind, beastly,
savage, wicked
The old witch was **cruel** to
the princess.

crumb (n)
morsel, flake, scrap, speck, smidgeon
The ogre didn't leave a single **crumb**
of bread for anyone else.

crumble (v)
fall apart, disintegrate, collapse,
decay
Vampires **crumble** to dust in
the sunlight.

crush (v)
smash, destroy, break, shatter,
mash, squash, squeeze, grind,
trample, pound, pulverize
The giant will **crush** the rocks
underfoot.

cry (n)
screech, scream, call, shout,
yell, bellow
Leo heard a loud **cry** from the forest.

cry (v)
weep, sob, wail, howl, bawl, snivel,
blub, whimper, burst into tears,
shed tears
Don't **cry** – it will stop hurting soon.

cuddle (v)
hug, hold, clasp, snuggle, embrace
Cuddle the baby to stop her crying.

curved (adj)
wavy, bent, twisted, twisty, coiled,
swirly, curled, curly
The bird has a **curved** beak.

cut (n)
gash, graze, nick, scrape, wound
I need a plaster because there is
a **cut** on my knee.

cut (v)
1. gash, scratch, nick, stab, hurt
You will **cut** your finger if you play
with knives.

2. chop, dice, slice
Please **cut** the vegetables into small
pieces.

3. amputate, remove
The surgeon will have to **cut off**
his arm.

4. slash, hack away, fell, remove
The gardener will **cut down** the
brambles and nettles.

5. trim, snip, shorten
Mum will **cut** my hair tomorrow.

Dd

damp (adj)

soggy, moist, wet, soaked, waterlogged
My clothes are **damp** from the rain.

dance (v)

skip, boogie, waltz, bop
We love to **dance** around the room.

dangerous (adj)

unsafe, harmful, unhealthy, risky,
perilous, dodgy
Playing with fire is a **dangerous**
thing to do.

daring (adj)

brave, courageous, bold,
fearless, plucky
The **daring** soldier rushed into battle.
opposite: *timid*

dark (adj)

1. gloomy, dim, overcast, shadowy,
black, dingy, murky
It was a **dark** and stormy night.
opposite: *light*
2. deep
My coat is **dark** green.

dash (v)

rush, run, hurry, race, sprint, hurtle
We had to **dash** to the bus stop
because the bus was coming.

dead (adj)

lifeless, deceased, late
There was a **dead** fox on the road.
opposite: *alive*

decide (v)

choose, pick, select
You can **decide** which cake to have.

decorate (v)

adorn, do up, brighten, ornament
I bought paint to **decorate** my
bedroom.

definitely

certainly, surely, clearly, obviously
It will **definitely** rain later.

a
b
c
d
e
f
g
h
i
j
k
l
m
n
o
p
q
r
s
t
u
v
w
x
y
z

a
b
c
d
e
f
g
h
i
j
k
l
m
n
o
p
q
r
s
t
u
v
w
x
y
z

deliberately

on purpose, intentionally, knowingly
The girl hurt me **deliberately**.
opposite: *accidentally*

delicious (adj)

tasty, yummy, scrummy, scrumptious
Matilda asked for more of the **delicious** pudding.

delight (n)

joy, pleasure
Ava's new puppy is a **delight**.

den (n)

1. lair, nest, burrow, hole
The fox hid in its **den**.

2. shelter, hideaway, hidey-hole
Ibrahim built a **den** in the bushes.

desert (n)

bush, wilderness, wasteland
The sun beat down as Florence rode her camel across the **desert**.

desert (v)

1. abandon, leave, give up
The knight had to **desert** the castle he was guarding.

2. abandon, maroon, leave, strand
The pirates planned to **desert** the boy on an island.

die (v)

1. perish, stop living, expire
You will **die** if you drink that poison.
opposite: *live*

2. become extinct, disappear
Pandas will **die out** if we don't help them.

different (adj)

1. alternative, another
Choose a **different** book.

2. unlike, opposite, unequal
The sisters are very **different** from each other.

3. varied, various, dissimilar
There are four **different** sorts of fish.

difficult (adj)

1. hard, tricky, tough, challenging, puzzling, baffling, complicated
This test is too **difficult** for me.
opposite: *easy*

2. disobedient, troublesome, awkward
The **difficult** boy would not listen to his mother.

dig (v)

burrow, tunnel, excavate
The rabbit will **dig** under the lawn.

dim (adj)

murky, dull, gloomy, dark, shadowy
The room was so **dim** that Lucy could
not read the sign.

dirty (adj)

1. soiled, grimy, filthy, grubby, muddy
Please clean those **dirty** boots!
opposite: *clean*

2. polluted, cloudy, unclean
That water is **dirty** so don't drink it.

disappear (v)

vanish, leave, fade away, depart
The genie **disappeared** after
Aladdin's third wish.
opposite: *appear*

discover (v)

1. find, locate, track down, spot,
come upon
The children will **discover** the
treasure if they follow the map.

2. reveal, uncover, unearth
Our secret was **discovered**.

disease (n)

illness, sickness, bug, infection
She caught a **disease** from her sister.

disgusting (adj)

vile, foul, horrible, nasty, loathsome
The dragon's breath was **disgusting**.

display (v)

show, exhibit, show off, reveal,
present
You can **display** your artwork in
the classroom.

do (v)

1. complete, finish, carry out,
perform, get done, deal with,
take care of
I have a lot to **do** before I leave.

2. act, behave
Be careful what you **do**.

3. fasten, button, zip up
Do up your coat.

a
b
c
d
e
f
g
h
i
j
k
l
m
n
o
p
q
r
s
t
u
v
w
x
y
z

dot (n)

spot, splash, fleck, splatter, dab, drop
There is a **dot** of paint on your shoe.

drag (v)

pull, haul, tug, yank, tow
Drag that box over here.

draw (v)

sketch, doodle
I like to **draw** pictures of flowers.

dread (v)

fear, shudder, tremble
I **dread** to think what my teacher
will say.

dreadful (adj)

1. awful, terrible, horrible
I had a **dreadful** day at school.

2. terrifying, ghastly, hideous, grim,
horrendous, frightful
There is a **dreadful** monster round
the corner.

drip (v)

dribble, drizzle, drop, trickle
The water will **drip** from the hole
in the pipe.
opposite: *pour*

dull (adj)

dreary, boring, humdrum, tedious
The gardening programme was **dull**.

dumb (adj)

1. mute, unable to speak, silent,
speechless
The girl was struck **dumb**.

2. stupid, dense, thick
Stop asking **dumb** questions.
opposite: *clever*

Ee

eager (adj)
keen, enthusiastic
Layla is **eager** to learn the guitar.
opposite: *unenthusiastic*

early
promptly, in good time
Henry got up **early** to go swimming.
opposite: *late*

earth (n)
soil, dirt, ground, land
The lizard scuttled over the **earth**.

easy (adj)
simple, straightforward, undemanding
That question is **easy** to answer.
opposite: *difficult*

eat (v)
consume, devour, gobble up, scoff, snaffle, snap up, munch, nibble
The dog will **eat** the food if you leave it there.

empty (adj)
1. uninhabited, vacant, unoccupied, deserted, abandoned
The neighbours moved out and left the house **empty**.
opposite: *full*
2. hollow
The chocolate rabbit was **empty** on the inside.

end (n)
back, rear, tail
Molly joined the **end** of the queue.
opposite: *front*

end (v)
finish, complete, stop, close, conclude
You must **end** your game immediately.

ending (n)
finish, conclusion, close
The **ending** of the story is sad.
opposite: *beginning*

endless (adj)
eternal, unending, ceaseless, everlasting, limitless, constant
The witch cast an **endless** curse on the prince.

enemy (n)
foe, rival, opponent
The giant's **enemy** chased him with a sword.

a
b
c
d
e
f
g
h
i
j
k
l
m
n
o
p
q
r
s
t
u
v
w
x
y
z

enjoy

a
b
c
d
e
f
g
h
i
j
k
l
m
n
o
p
q
r
s
t
u
v
w
x
y
z

enjoy (v)
take pleasure in, love, revel in, relish, appreciate
Sadie really **enjoys** riding horses.

enormous (adj)
huge, gigantic, colossal, immense, vast
There is an **enormous** elephant at the zoo.
opposite: *tiny*

enough
sufficient, plenty, adequate, ample
We have **enough** plates for everyone.
opposite: *insufficient*

entirely
completely, wholly, altogether, totally, utterly, thoroughly
I've **entirely** forgotten what I was going to say.
opposite: *partly*

equal (adj)
equivalent, the same, matching, identical, even
The two portions are **equal** in size.
opposite: *uneven*

error (n)
mistake, miscalculation
He made an **error** and got the sum wrong.

even (adj)
1. equal, level, the same, identical
The scores of the two teams are **even**.
2. level, smooth, flat, straight
The surface of the tennis court must be completely **even**.
opposite: *uneven*

eventually
finally, at last, in the end
The spell will wear off **eventually**.

evil (adj)
wicked, cruel, villainous
The **evil** queen poisoned Snow White.
opposite: *good*

excellent (adj)
exceptional, fantastic, great, super, superb, fabulous, wonderful, outstanding, top, brilliant
The film was **excellent** – I want to watch it again right now!
opposite: *dreadful*

exciting (adj)
thrilling, gripping, sensational, heart-stopping, lively, action-packed
Lucas went on an **exciting** fairground ride.
opposite: *boring*

exercise (n)

1. task, question, lesson
The students did the second **exercise** in the book.

2. activity, sport, training, workout
You must do some **exercise** to stay healthy.

expect (v)

guess, anticipate, forecast, believe, imagine, assume, suspect, presume
I **expect** it will rain on holiday.

expensive (adj)

costly, dear, high-priced, pricey, over-priced
That car is too **expensive** to buy.
opposite: *cheap*

extra (adj)

additional, further, supplementary, bonus, more
There will be **extra** cake on Fridays.

extraordinary (adj)

1. amazing, exceptional, remarkable, outstanding, terrific
The boy has made **extraordinary** progress this term.

2. unusual, special, bizarre, odd, uncommon
We saw an **extraordinary** bird in the garden.
opposite: *ordinary*

a
b
c
d
e
f
g
h
i
j
k
l
m
n
o
p
q
r
s
t
u
v
w
x
y
z

Ff

faint (adj)

1. dim, faded, pale, hazy, unclear, slight, indistinct
There is a **faint** scratch on the table.

2. dizzy, light-headed, giddy, unstable, shaky, weak, wobbly
She felt **faint** and had to sit down.

fair (adj)

1. just, honest, generous, decent
It's **fair** to share your sweets equally.

2. blonde, golden, pale, light
She has **fair** hair and blue eyes.

fairly

1. quite, rather, reasonably, moderately
It's **fairly** early and not many people are awake.

2. equally, evenly
The teacher shared the packet of sweets **fairly** so we each had seven.

fake (adj)

imitation, forged, phoney, mock, bogus
The merchant sold the old man a **fake** magic carpet that didn't fly.
opposite: *genuine*

fall (n)

1. tumble, accident
My granny had a **fall** and broke her ankle.

2. drop, decrease, reduction
There has been a sharp **fall** in the number of pupils playing tennis.
opposite: *rise*

fall (v)

1. topple, tumble
If you lean out of the window, you might **fall**!

2. plummet, drop, plunge
The rocks might **fall** down the cliff in windy weather.

3. trip, stumble, slip
If you leave your shoes on the stairs, people will **fall** over them.

4. drop, reduce, slump
The price of chocolate eggs will **fall** after Easter.

false (adj)

1. fake, artificial, pretend
The pirate walked with a limp because he had a **false** leg.
2. untrue, incorrect, wrong, bogus, faulty
Carrots are blue – true or **false**?
opposite: *true*

famous (adj)

well-known, renowned, leading, famed, acclaimed
We were really excited about the **famous** footballer visiting our school.
opposite: *unknown*

fan (n)

supporter, devotee, follower
He is a **fan** of his local rugby club and goes to every game.

fancy (adj)

elaborate, ornate, decorated, lavish
She wore a **fancy** outfit covered in sequins to the carnival.
opposite: *plain*

fantastic (adj)

amazing, incredible, superb, stupendous, unbelievable, fabulous, brilliant, stonking
We went on a **fantastic** holiday to Bali.

far

distant, remote, a long way away
The magic cave is **far** from here – we will have to walk all night.

fashionable (adj)

trendy, chic, stylish, up-to-date, cool
My aunt always wears **fashionable** clothes.

fast (adj)

1. quick, speedy, rapid, hasty, high-speed
We went in a **fast** car so it didn't take long.
2. brisk, swift
We went for a **fast** walk that made me out of breath.
opposite: *slow*

fast

1. speedily, quickly, rapidly, swiftly, briskly, hastily
The horse galloped **fast** to the finishing line.
2. securely, firmly, tightly
The kitten was stuck **fast** in the pipe.
3. deeply, soundly
The baby is **fast** asleep.

fasten (v)

fix, fit, attach
Fasten the hook securely to the wall.

a
b
c
d
e
f
g
h
i
j
k
l
m
n
o
p
q
r
s
t
u
v
w
x
y
z

fat (n)

grease, lard
I prefer to cut the **fat** from my meat before I eat it.

fat (adj)

large, overweight, chubby, podgy, tubby, dumpy, obese, plump, stout, heavy, chunky, hefty
The dog was too **fat** for its basket.
opposite: *thin*

faulty (adj)

broken, damaged, defective, imperfect, unsound, out of order
The lamp is **faulty** so don't use it.

favourite (adj)

best, preferred, favoured, best-loved, number-one
Which is your **favourite** flavour of ice cream?

fear (n)

dread, horror, terror
I have a **fear** of slugs.

fear (v)

dread, worry about, panic about, be concerned about, be frightened of, be afraid of, be scared of
I **fear** being locked outside in the cold.

feast (n)

banquet, spread, dinner
The king invited the people to a grand **feast**.

feel (v)

1. sense, think, believe, suspect
I **feel** you don't like me.

2. touch, stroke, handle
Do you want to **feel** the snake's skin?

fetch (v)

bring, retrieve, go for, obtain
Netta ran off to **fetch** her doll.

field (n)

1. meadow, pasture, plain
There are four cows in the **field**.

2. pitch, court, ground, area
The sportsman ran across the **field**.

fierce (adj)

ferocious, violent, vicious, savage
The **fierce** monster scared the child.

fight (n)

1. battle, conflict, war, clash, confrontation, skirmish
The soldiers had a **fight** in a field.

2. scuffle, argument, quarrel, row, squabble, scrap, tiff, feud
When I have a **fight** with my friend, we always make up afterwards.

fight (v)

1. battle, struggle, protest, argue, dispute, negotiate
We had to **fight** for the right to have a longer holiday.

2. attack, duel with, clash with, assault
The warrior had to **fight** the goblin.

fill (v)

cram, pack, load, overload, stuff
Let's **fill** the shopping trolley with toys.

filled (adj)

blocked, clogged, plugged, bunged up
The drain is **filled** with hair.

finally

eventually, in the end, ultimately, at last
We **finally** arrived home at midnight and went straight to bed.

find (v)

1. locate, discover, spot, come across, uncover, encounter, track down
Can you **find** the hidden word in the puzzle?

2. discover, learn
Later, we will **find out** if we have won the competition.

fine (adj)

very well, great, OK, all right
I'm **fine**, thank you, and how are you?

finish (n)

end, ending, close, conclusion
We stayed until the **finish** of the race.
opposite: *start, beginning*

finish (v)

1. end, close, conclude, stop
The show will **finish** in ten minutes.
opposite: *start, commence*

2. complete
You must **finish** your dinner before going out.

a
b
c
d
e
f
g
h
i
j
k
l
m
n
o
p
q
r
s
t
u
v
w
x
y
z

a
b
c
d
e
f
g
h
i
j
k
l
m
n
o
p
q
r
s
t
u
v
w
x
y
z

firm (adj)

1. stiff, hard, solid
The ground was **firm** underfoot so it was easy to run.

2. strict, determined, unbending, inflexible
The teacher was very **firm** and didn't let the children talk in class.

first (adj)

earliest, original
The **first** car was made more than 100 years ago.

fix (v)

1. mend, repair, sort out, put right,
We had to **fix** the faulty cooker before we could make dinner.

2. arrange, pick, choose, settle on
Let's **fix** a day for your party.

3. join, fit, connect, link, fasten
He must **fix** these two parts together.

fizzy (adj)

bubbly, sparkling, gassy, carbonated, foaming
Eva likes **fizzy** water with her lunch.
opposite: *flat, still*

flap (n)

state, tizzy, fluster, strop, fuss
Mum got in a **flap** about my ruined coat.

flap (v)

flutter, shake, wave
The flag will **flap** in the wind.

flat (adj)

1. even, smooth, level
The land was completely **flat** so we could see for miles.

2. dull, unvarying, monotonous, boring
The teacher spoke in a **flat** voice, which made her pupils fall asleep.

3. deflated, punctured
My bike has a **flat** tyre.

fly (v)

soar, hover, glide, swoop, drift, flap, flutter
The birds **fly** high above us.

follow (v)

pursue, tail, track, shadow, trail, chase
The police will **follow** the robbers back to their house.

fool (v)

trick, dupe, deceive, con
You can't **fool** us with that disguise!

foolish (adj)

mad, crazy, insane, idiotic, ridiculous, silly, stupid, unwise
Running next to the swimming pool is a **foolish** thing to do.

forever

always, eternally, permanently, without end, endlessly, for good
The dodos are gone **forever**.

friend (n)

mate, pal, chum, buddy, companion
I sat next to my **friend**.

opposite: *enemy*

fright (n)

1. shock, surprise, scare
The ghost gave me a **fright**.

2. horror, fear, terror, dread, panic
She shivered in **fright**.

frighten (v)

scare, alarm, startle, shock, terrify
Jo **frightened** his friend by screaming.

frightening (adj)

scary, terrifying, alarming, horrifying, horrific
The ghost ride at the fair is really **frightening**.

frown (v)

scowl, glare, glower, grimace
We all **frowned** at the naughty boy.

opposite: *smile*

full (adj)

filled, full up, chock-a-block
Ella's fridge is **full** of food.

fun (adj)

1. amusing, enjoyable, entertaining, pleasant
We always have a **fun** time when we go to the zoo.

funny (adj)

1. amusing, humorous, hilarious
The jokes in that book are very **funny**.

2. strange, odd, unfamiliar, weird, bizarre, peculiar, unusual, curious
I have a **funny** feeling in my tummy.

a b c d e f g h i j k l m n o p q r s t u v w x y z

a
b
c
d
e
f
g
h
i
j
k
l
m
n
o
p
q
r
s
t
u
v
w
x
y
z

furry (adj)

hairy, fuzzy, fluffy, bushy, shaggy, woolly
The monster was green and **furry**.

fussy (adj)

1. choosy, picky, nit-picking, demanding, precise, exacting
Nina is very **fussy** about her food.

2. ornate, prissy, fiddly, detailed
The little girl wore a **fussy** dress covered with frills and bows.

fuzzy (adj)

hairy, furry, fluffy
He picked up a **fuzzy** caterpillar.

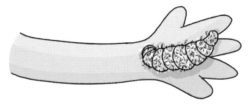

Gg

gang (n)

group, company, band, tribe, crew, clan, troop, circle
We have a good **gang** of friends.

gap (n)

hole, crack, crevice, break, breach, opening, cleft, cranny, space
There is a **gap** in the wall that I can just squeeze through.

gentle (adj)

tender, careful, kind, attentive
The boy was **gentle** with the little baby.

get (v)

See page 125

ghost (n)

spirit, ghoul, phantom, spectre
There is a **ghost** in the haunted castle.

giant (adj)

huge, enormous, gigantic, immense, monstrous, mammoth, vast
Harry's mum made him a **giant** cake for his birthday.

give (v)

1. pass, hand over, present
Give the book to me and I'll read it to you.

2. offer, present, donate, provide, grant
Daniel wants to **give** money to a charity for sick animals.

give back (v)

return, restore, hand over
When will you **give back** that book you borrowed?

glad (adj)

pleased, happy, relieved, thrilled, delighted, cheerful, overjoyed
She is **glad** her dog has come home.

gloomy (adj)

1. dim, dark, shadowy, murky
It was hard to see where to go in the **gloomy** forest.

2. miserable, depressed, glum, blue, down, melancholy
Mia felt really **gloomy** when she heard the party was cancelled.
opposite: *happy*

glow (v)

gleam, glimmer, shine
The hot coals **glow** in the fireplace.

go (v)

See page 126

good (adj)

1. kind, considerate, caring, thoughtful
It was **good** of Harvey to help the injured bird.

2. suitable, ideal, fine
It is a **good** day for a picnic.

3. obedient, cooperative, well-behaved
Jessica is always **good** when she visits her granny.

4. interesting, exciting, respected, worthwhile, well-paid
My mum has a **good** job.

gossip (n)

chatter, rumours, chat, idle talk
You shouldn't believe the **gossip** you hear.

a
b
c
d
e
f
g
h
i
j
k
l
m
n
o
p
q
r
s
t
u
v
w
x
y
z

a
b
c
d
e
f
g
h
i
j
k
l
m
n
o
p
q
r
s
t
u
v
w
x
y
z

grab (v)

1. grip, grasp, take hold of, seize
Jonny had to **grab** the handle to stop himself from falling.

2. snatch, take, pick up
You can **grab** a snack on the way out.

grand (adj)

impressive, magnificent, stately, splendid
Cinderella went to a **grand** ball.

great (adj)

1. huge, large, enormous, massive, gigantic, colossal, immense
Evie tipped the toys into a **great** heap.

2. wonderful, super, fabulous, superb, fantastic, brilliant, excellent, terrific
She had a **great** time on the school trip.

3. talented, brilliant, first-rate, leading, important, skilful
Everyone went to see the exhibition by the **great** artist.

greedy (adj)

voracious, ravenous, gluttonous
The **greedy** boy ate twelve roast chickens!

grey (adj)

silver
My great granddad has **grey** hair.

grim (adj)

serious, severe, sullen, stern
The judge looked **grim** as he faced the prisoner.

grip (v)

grasp, clasp, clutch, clench, hold, grab
The children must **grip** the rope and slide down the bank.

ground (n)

floor, land, earth
Don't drop litter on the **ground** – throw it in the bin.

group (n)

1. gang, crowd, band, troop, bunch
There is a noisy **group** of boys by the gate.

2. collection, set
My aunt has a **group** of china jugs on the shelf.

3. club, society, organization, association
I went to a music **group** to play the piano.

grow (v)

1. expand, increase in size, enlarge, inflate, swell, fill out
If you eat your food, you will **grow**.

2. thrive, flourish, develop, survive
The tree will **grow** best in sunlight.

3. become, turn
The queen will **grow** wiser as she ages.

4. mature, become adult, age
What will you do when you **grow up**?

grumble (v)

complain, grouch, whinge, object, fret, whine, moan
Sit still and don't **grumble** about being hungry!

grumpy (adj)

grouchy, ill-tempered, irritable, bad-tempered, sullen, sulky, crabby, surly
The **grumpy** man complained about the noise.
opposite: *cheerful*

guard (v)

protect, look after, cover, defend, oversee, shield, preserve
The man's job was to **guard** the castle.

guide (v)

lead, escort, steer, show, pilot, shepherd
Daisy's dog will **guide** her across the road.

guilty (adj)

1. responsible, blameworthy, culpable, in the wrong
He was put on trial and found **guilty**.

2. ashamed, sorry, remorseful
Charlotte felt **guilty** even though she had done nothing wrong.

a b c d e f g h i j k l m n o p q r s t u v w x y z

Hh

hairy (adj)
furry, fuzzy, shaggy, bristly
The troll had a **hairy** back.

hang (v)
suspend (from), attach (to)
Please **hang** the picture on
that wall over there.

happy (adj)
1. pleased, thrilled, delighted, glad,
overjoyed
I'd be **happy** to come to your party.
opposite: *unhappy*

2. jolly, joyful, merry, enjoyable
My cousin's wedding was a
happy occasion.
opposite: *sad*

hard (adj)
1. difficult, taxing, tough, tricky,
demanding
It's a **hard** choice whether to go to
Erin's party or Lucy's.
opposite: *easy, simple*

2. stiff, firm, rigid, solid
The concrete has gone **hard** so it's
fine to walk on.
opposite: *soft*

hardly
barely, only just, scarcely
Grandma had **hardly** sat down when
the doorbell rang.

harm (v)
hurt, injure, damage
Paddling in the cold water won't
harm you.

hate (v)
dislike, detest, can't bear, can't stand
I really **hate** cabbage.
opposite: *love*

have (v)
See page 126

head (n)
1. skull
Don't bump your **head** on the ceiling.

2. leader, boss, captain, chief,
commander
Captain Redbeard was the **head**
of a band of pirates.

head (v)
1. lead, run, manage, organize
A scientist will **head** the expedition
to the North Pole.

2. go to, make for, go towards,
approach
We always **head for** the beach when
it is hot.

a b c d e f g h i j k l m n o p q r s t u v w x y z

head (adj)

main, lead, chief, principal
The **head** pirate waved his sword.

healthy (adj)

1. in good health, fine, well, able-bodied, flourishing, robust, sound, vigorous
My grandmother is **healthy** even though she is old.
opposite: *sick*

2. nutritious, good for you
Fruit is a **healthy** snack.
opposite: *unhealthy*

3. vigorous, brisk, stout, strong, tough
Frankie gave the carpet a **healthy** beating.
opposite: *gentle*

heat (v)

warm, cook
Heat the curry in the microwave.

heavy (adj)

1. weighty, hefty, bulky
The suitcase was too **heavy** to carry.
opposite: *light*

2. overweight, fat, chunky, obese, stout, well-built
There was a **heavy** man in the way.
opposite: *thin, slim*

help (n)

1. assistance, advice, support, tips
Luca's dad gave him some **help** with his homework.

2. benefit, plus, advantage, useful, good thing, bonus
It's a **help** in this job if you know something about animals.

help (v)

assist, aid, give a hand
Please **help** me to lift this heavy box.

helpful (adj)

useful, constructive, beneficial
It's **helpful** to know where you're going before you set off.

helpless (adj)

powerless, unprotected, weak, vulnerable, defenceless
The kitten was **helpless** without its mother.

a
b
c
d
e
f
g
h
i
j
k
l
m
n
o
p
q
r
s
t
u
v
w
x
y
z

a
b
c
d
e
f
g
h
i
j
k
l
m
n
o
p
q
r
s
t
u
v
w
x
y
z

hidden (adj)

concealed, covered, cloaked, screened, made invisible

The **hidden** door was covered by climbing roses.

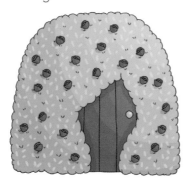

hide (v)

conceal, bury, stash, smuggle, stow

The villain tried to **hide** the jewels under his velvet cloak.

high (adj)

1. tall, towering, looming, lofty

The goat climbed a **high** mountain.

2. shrill, piercing, squeaky

The singer sang in a **high** voice.

opposite: *low*

hill (n)

mound, knoll, rise, slope, mount, hillock

Jack and Jill went up a **hill**.

hit (v)

1. strike, knock, bump into, crash into

Be careful not to **hit** the post.

2. punch, thump, bash, wallop, smack, slap, whack, beat

Don't **hit** your sister!

hold (v)

grip, grasp, clasp, clench, clutch

You have to **hold** the handrail to go up the stairs.

honest (adj)

truthful, decent, honourable, virtuous, trustworthy

The **honest** boy told his mother the truth.

opposite: *dishonest*

horrible (adj)

foul, terrible, rank, disgusting, awful

Eggs smell **horrible** when they are rotten.

horrify (v)

appal, disgust, upset, dismay, alarm, shock, sicken, outrage
The sight of the huge snake was enough to **horrify** her.

hot (adj)

scorching, baking, burning, scalding, blistering, warm, heated
The potato was **hot** when it came out of the oven.

house (n)

home, place, abode
The rich man's **house** had fifty bedrooms.

hug (n)

cuddle, squeeze, embrace
The girls give each other a **hug**.

huge (adj)

enormous, gigantic, immense, vast
A whale is **huge** compared with a human.
opposite: *minute, tiny*

hum (v)

buzz, rumble, throb, drone, whirr
You can tell the fridge is on because you can hear it **hum**.

hungry (adj)

starving, ravenous, peckish, famished
Have a snack, or you might be **hungry** later.

hurry (v)

be quick, make haste, be speedy, get a move on, rush, dash
Hurry! You need to catch the bus.

hurt (v)

1. harm, injure, damage
Syed will **hurt** the hamster if he holds it too tightly.

2. ache, be painful, be sore
I have to go to the doctor because my head **hurts**.

hurtful (adj)

mean, spiteful, unkind, upsetting, destructive, nasty
Grace is crying because her sister has said something **hurtful**.

hut (n)

shed, shack, hovel, cabin, shelter
The shepherd's **hut** is warm and cosy.

a b c d e f g h i j k l m n o p q r s t u v w x y z

a
b
c
d
e
f
g
h
i
j
k
l
m
n
o
p
q
r
s
t
u
v
w
x
y
z

Ii

icy (adj)

freezing, sub-zero, frosty, chilly, bitterly cold
It is **icy** outside today.

ill (adj)

sick, unwell, poorly, infected, unhealthy, sickly
Caitlin stayed in bed because she was **ill**.
opposite: *well*

illustration (n)

picture, diagram, image
There are beautiful **illustrations** in this book.

imaginary (adj)

make-believe, unreal, pretend, made-up
The princess waved an **imaginary** wand at the frog.
opposite: *real*

immediately

instantly, straight away, promptly, directly, without stopping
The little pig went to the door **immediately** when the wolf knocked.

important (adj)

1. essential, vital, necessary, crucial
It is **important** that you know what to do if there's a fire.

2. first-class, well-known, famous, top, high-ranking
Mum is an **important** scientist.

increase (v)

grow, rise, multiply, swell
The number of people in the world will **increase** over time.
opposite: *decrease*

incredible (adj)

1. unbelievable, implausible,
far-fetched, improbable, unlikely
The prisoner told an **incredible** story.

2. fantastic, amazing, wonderful,
stupendous, superb, brilliant
We had an **incredible** time
on holiday.
opposite: *terrible*

inside (n)

1. interior
She painted the **inside** of the
box blue.
opposite: *outside*

2. guts, internal organs,
intestines, stomach
Jake's **insides** churned at the thought
of the scary ride.

inside

1. within, in, into
Lexi put the small mouse **inside**
the box to keep it safe.

2. indoors
The children had to play **inside**
because of the rain.
opposite: *outside*

instantly

immediately, straight away, at once,
right away
The genie appeared **instantly** when
Aladdin rubbed the lamp.

interested (adj)

keen on, crazy about, obsessed with,
into, fascinated by
My little sister is **interested**
in aeroplanes.

interesting (adj)

fascinating, enthralling, captivating,
absorbing
I saw an **interesting** programme
about sharks.
opposite: *boring*

invent (v)

create, develop, design, come up with
I am planning to **invent** a new type
of aeroplane.

item (n)

1. object, thing
Liam bought the **item** in the market.

2. bit, piece, component
There is one **item** missing from
the game.

a
b
c
d
e
f
g
h
i
j
k
l
m
n
o
p
q
r
s
t
u
v
w
x
y
z

Jj

jail (n)

prison, cell, dungeon, lock-up
The criminal broke out of the **jail**.

jerk (v)

tug, yank, wrench, jolt
The baby **jerked** the pull-along car.

job (n)

1. work, occupation, career, trade
profession, employment
What type of **job** do you want to do
when you're older?

2. task, chore, activity, assignment
Your next **job** is to wash up.

jog (v)

1. jolt, bash, nudge, shake,
jostle, bump
Don't **jog** me when I'm painting!

2. run, trot
We decided to **jog** to town.

join (v)

1. connect, link, stick, attach
Let's **join** the balloons together
with string.

2. belong to, sign up for, enrol in,
become a member of, enlist in,
register with
Carl wants to **join** the hockey club.

joke (n)

1. prank, trick, jape, laugh
Don't cry – it was just a **joke**.

2. gag, one-liner
My uncle always tells corny **jokes**.

jolly (adj)

1. cheery, cheerful, good-humoured, carefree, jovial, merry
The **jolly** captain sailed the boat across the sea.
opposite: *miserable, gloomy*

2. quite, rather, fairly
It is **jolly** cold outside.

journey (n)

trip, voyage, outing, jaunt, tour, expedition, safari, trek
I went on a **journey** to Egypt with my aunt.

joy (n)

pleasure, cheer, bliss, delight, glee, happiness
My cousin takes great **joy** in her singing.
opposite: *sorrow*

joyful (adj)

cheerful, happy, blissful, gleeful
The wedding was a **joyful** occasion.
opposite: *sad, miserable*

judge (v)

decide, assess, consider, determine, choose
You will have to **judge** who is the better dancer.

jumble (n)

mix, mishmash, confusion, muddle
There is always a huge **jumble** of shoes outside the soft play centre.

jump (v)

1. leap, bound, vault, skip, lunge, pounce
The kangaroo could easily **jump** over the ditch.

2. start, be startled (by), be surprised (by)
When the snake appeared it made me **jump**.

just (adj)

fair, honest, reasonable, true, unbiased
The king gave a **just** ruling and let the knight go free.
opposite: *unfair*

just

1. barely, scarcely, hardly, recently, this moment
Don't ask Mum questions – she has only **just** arrived home.

2. only, but, exactly
There is **just** one pie left so we will have to share it.

a
b
c
d
e
f
g
h
i
j
k
l
m
n
o
p
q
r
s
t
u
v
w
x
y
z

Kk

keen (adj)

1. enthusiastic, eager, devoted, committed, zealous
Isabella is a **keen** skater and practises every week.

2. eager, anxious, impatient
Ben is **keen** to start at his new school.
opposite: *reluctant*

keep (v)

1. retain, hold on to, hang on to, own
You can **keep** that coat – it doesn't fit me.

2. store, leave, stash, stow
We **keep** the shoes by the door.

3. carry on, continue, go on, persist in, maintain
Keep running – we're nearly there!

4. last, survive, stay fresh
Will this sandwich **keep** until next Thursday?

5. delay, detain, hold up, make late
Hurry back – don't let them **keep** you.

kidnap (v)

seize, hold hostage, grab, abduct snatch, capture
The bandits tried to **kidnap** a shepherd boy.

kill (v)

destroy, annihilate, wipe out, slay, do away with, slaughter, murder
This trap will **kill** the slugs.

kind (n)

sort, type, flavour, variety, brand, make
What **kind** of ice cream do you like best?

kind (adj)

generous, giving, warm-hearted, considerate, thoughtful
My granny is very **kind** and never gets cross.
opposite: *unkind, mean*

kit (n)

1. uniform, clothes, gear, outfit
Boaz took his football **kit** to school.

2. tools, apparatus
Frances bought a **kit** for fixing her bicycle.

knock (n)

1. rap, hammering, bang, tap, pounding
There was a loud **knock** at the door.

2. bump, hit, blow, bash, bang, thump
I had a nasty **knock** on the head.

knock (v)

1. rap, tap
Please **knock** before you enter.

2. overturn, tip up, bump
Don't **knock over** that vase!

know (v)

1. understand, have knowledge of
How do you **know** so much about trains?

2. recognize, be acquainted with, be familiar with
Do you **know** Mr Watts?

knowledge (n)

1. information, learning, wisdom, details, facts, know-how
Amy picked up a lot of local **knowledge** during her time in Africa.

2. understanding, grasp, command, familiarity with
Seth has a good **knowledge** of Spanish.

Ll

lack (n)

shortage, scarcity, shortfall
There is a **lack** of seating in the hall.
opposite: *plenty*

land (n)

1. ground, property, space
There is some empty **land** next to the house, where children like playing.

2. earth, soil, ground
The **land** is very fertile in this area, so it's easy to grow things.

3. country, kingdom, state, nation
The children went to a **land** full of fairies.

land (v)

1. touch down, descend
The helicopter couldn't **land** in the storm.
opposite: *take off*

2. settle, alight, come to rest
Dragonflies like to **land** on reeds.

large (adj)

big, wide, long, huge, enormous, great, vast, colossal, gaping
There is a **large** hole in my jumper, so I can't wear it.

a
b
c
d
e
f
g
h
i
j
k
l
m
n
o
p
q
r
s
t
u
v
w
x
y
z

a
b
c
d
e
f
g
h
i
j
k
l
m
n
o
p
q
r
s
t
u
v
w
x
y
z

last (v)

continue, carry on, be sustained
This good weather won't **last** – it's going to rain tomorrow.

last (adj)

1. final, remaining, ultimate
Don't take the **last** cake!
opposite: *first*

2. final, closing, ending, concluding
She read the **last** chapter of the book.
opposite: *opening*

3. most recent, latest, previous
I saw the **last** issue of that magazine.

laugh (v)

1. giggle, chortle, chuckle, snigger, guffaw, titter
We always **laugh** at Nathan's jokes.

2. mock, ridicule, tease, make fun of,
It's mean to **laugh at** people.

law (n)

rule, ruling, regulation
There is a **law** to protect children from unsafe toys.

lay (v)

1. set out, arrange
Dad will **lay** the table when dinner is cooked.

2. spread, stretch out, put down, place, position, arrange
Fran needs to **lay** the blanket over the chairs to make a tent.

lazy (adj)

idle, inactive, slack
The **lazy** leopard lay on a branch all day.
opposite: *energetic*

lead (v)

take, show, guide
The steward will **lead** you to your seat.

leader (n)

head, chief, commander, boss
The man with the red hat is the **leader**.

leap (v)

jump, vault, spring, bound
The goat can **leap** from rock to rock.

learn (v)

master, pick up, acquire, understand
You will never **learn** to play the drums if you don't practise.

leave (v)

1. depart, set off, embark, go out
Put on your shoes – it's time to **leave**!

2. abandon, desert, ditch
Uncle Tom **left** his family and sailed round the world.

let (v)

1. allow, give permission to, permit
Mum **let** me eat the last biscuit.

2. release, free, drop
Don't **let go of** the dog's lead!

level (n)

1. stage, grade
Scarlett got to **level** twenty-five in the new game.

2. floor, storey
We parked on **level** six of the multi-storey car park.

level (adj)

flat, even, horizontal, straight
The boys looked for a **level** surface to use their roller skates.
opposite: *uneven*

lie (v)

lounge, recline, flop, stretch out, rest, sprawl
The cat will **lie** on the cushion all day if you let her.

life (n)

1. existence, being, lifestyle
The king has an easy **life** because he doesn't have to work.

2. survival
Don't disturb me unless it's a matter of **life** and death.

3. liveliness, vitality, energy, spirit, vigour
My granny is full of **life**.

lift (v)

raise, pick up, heft
I can **lift** this heavy box.

light (adj)

1. bright, sunny, well-lit
It gets **light** early in the summer.
opposite: *gloomy, dark*

2. small, dainty, simple
She ate a **light** lunch of pasta salad.
opposite: *hearty*

3. pale
My coat is **light** green.
opposite: *dark*

a
b
c
d
e
f
g
h
i
j
k
l
m
n
o
p
q
r
s
t
u
v
w
x
y
z

light (n)

1. lamp, bulb, lantern, torch
Turn on the **light** – it's getting dark.

2. brightness, daylight, glow, glare, glimmer, dazzle, flash, flicker, glint, gleam, shine
The **light** comes in through the curtains.

like (v)

1. enjoy, relish, favour, be fond of, appreciate, be keen on
Miriam **likes** garlic bread.
opposite: *dislike*

2. prefer
Mum **likes** us to take our shoes off when we come inside.

3. want, fancy
Would you **like** a biscuit?

like

1. as if, as though
It looks **like** it will rain.

2. similar to, identical to
That small dog is **like** a rat.

likely (adj)

probable, expected, predicted
It is **likely** that it will snow before the weekend.
opposite: *unlikely*

line (n)

1. rule, stripe, band, streak, bar, stroke
Draw a straight **line** across the page.

2. queue, column, chain, row
A **line** of people stretched down the road.

3. string, cord, wire, thread
Leah let the kite out on a long **line**.

4. boundary, edge, border
The workers drew a **line** round the area where they were planning to dig.

litter (n)

rubbish, garbage, waste, trash
Tyler picked up the **litter** the children had dropped.

little (adj)

1. short, brief, light
The baby has a **little** sleep after lunch.
opposite: *long*

2. tiny, small, minute, mini, micro, teeny-weeny
There is a **little** beetle on the floor.
opposite: *large*

live (v)

1. exist, survive, stay alive
Whales **live** for many years.

2. occupy, inhabit, reside in
We **live in** the ground-floor flat.

lively (adj)

1. active, alert, agile
The **lively** monkey climbed up
the tree.

2. bouncy, sprightly, jolly, merry,
quick, energetic
Granddad played a **lively** tune
on his violin.

lock (v)

fasten, secure, padlock, latch, bolt
Lock the shed door when you leave.

long (adj)

extended, lengthy, drawn-out
Freya waited a **long** time for a bus.
opposite: *short*

look (n)

1. stare, gaze, expression, glance
The teacher gave me a puzzled **look**.

2. appearance
I don't like the **look** of those
dark clouds.

look (v)

1. see, inspect, spy, examine,
watch, observe, stare at, peer at,
study, peep at
I like to **look** at spiders.

2. seems, appears
What's the matter with Arthur? He
looks ill.

3. resembles
That cat **looks like** a small tiger.

lot (n)

1. many, a great deal, plenty,
a great number, loads, tons
There will be **a lot** of children at
the party.
opposite: *few*

2. collection, set, batch, pile, load
Dad brought another **lot** of old
magazines down from the attic.

loud (adj)

noisy, deafening, blaring, piercing
The music was **loud** near the stage.
opposite: *quiet*

love (n)

1. affection, fondness, kind wishes
Granny says that she sends her **love**.

2. passion, devotion, adoration
The prince's **love** for the poor
shepherd girl was very strong.

a
b
c
d
e
f
g
h
i
j
k
l
m
n
o
p
q
r
s
t
u
v
w
x
y
z

a
b
c
d
e
f
g
h
i
j
k
l
m
n
o
p
q
r
s
t
u
v
w
x
y
z

love (v)

be crazy about, be mad about, adore, be fond of
Daniel **loves** his new sister, Maya.
opposite: *hate*

lovely (adj)

See page 127

luck (n)

1. fortune
Sebastian always has good **luck** – he wins every time.

2. accident, chance, fluke
Chloe went to the right door by **luck**.

luggage (n)

baggage, cases, bags, belongings
Adam left his **luggage** on the train.

lump (n)

1. chunk, blob, clot
There is a **lump** in my custard.

2. bump, bulge
I can see a **lump** under the bedclothes.

3. clump, wad, cluster, bunch, knot
The noodles have gone into a **lump**.

Mm

machine (n)

contraption, device, gadget, engine
Max invented a **machine** to turn mud into chocolate.

mad (adj)

1. crazy, bonkers, odd, nuts, loopy, eccentric
My Aunt Lily is totally **mad**.

2. crazy about, enthusiastic about, keen on, devoted to, hooked on
Sophie is **mad about** horses.

3. furious, angry, cross
When we throw things in class, it makes the teacher **mad**.

main (adj)

chief, principal, most important, key
Sludgy mashed potato was the **main** reason Jo didn't like school dinners.

mainly

mostly, chiefly, principally, largely
We go to town **mainly** by car.

make (n)

model, brand, kind, label (of clothes)
Which **make** of bicycle do you have?

make (v)

1. build, construct, put together, fabricate, assemble, form
My brother is planning to **make** a giant dinosaur from boxes.

2. cook, prepare, assemble
Dad will **make** lunch while I play football.

3. force, compel
You can't **make** me go to the shops!

manner (n)

1. type, sort, style
What **manner** of creature did you see?

2. behaviour, attitude
The dress designer adopted a snooty **manner**.

3. style, way, fashion
The shopkeeper piled up the books in a disorganized **manner**.

manners (n)

politeness, courtesy
My uncle doesn't teach his children any **manners**.

many (adj)

lots, tons, plenty, loads, heaps, stacks, hundreds, masses, a great deal, a great number
Many tourists queued up to see the Crown Jewels.
opposite: *few*

mark (n)

1. spot, stain, smear, smudge, blotch
There is a **mark** on Sara's new shirt.

2. grade, level, score, percentage
What **mark** did you get in your music test?

mark (v)

1. stain, smear, smudge, soil
Don't **mark** the curtains with your dirty fingers!

2. grade, assess
The teacher will **mark** the pupils' work at lunchtime.

marvellous (adj)

brilliant, wonderful, fantastic, stupendous, amazing
We made a **marvellous** model boat.

a
b
c
d
e
f
g
h
i
j
k
l
m
n
o
p
q
r
s
t
u
v
w
x
y
z

a
b
c
d
e
f
g
h
i
j
k
l
m
n
o
p
q
r
s
t
u
v
w
x
y
z

material (n)

1. fabric, cloth
The bear costume is made out of furry **material**.
See also page 123

2. information, facts, ideas, data
We are collecting **material** for an article in the school magazine.

3. stuff, components, parts, bits and pieces
We have all the **materials** to make a racing car.

matter (n)

problem, issue, situation, trouble, difficulty
What's the **matter** with your dog?

matter (v)

count, make a difference, be important
Does it **matter** if we run out of milk?

may (v)

is allowed to, is permitted to
Lucy **may** go to the park if she does her homework first.

mean (v)

1. signify, stand for, express, communicate
What does that word **mean**?

2. intend, plan
Riley didn't **mean** to break the glass.

mean (adj)

1. cruel, spiteful, harsh, unkind, nasty
The old witch was **mean** to her cat.
opposite: *kind*

2. stingy, miserly, tight
The prince was too **mean** to pay his servants properly.
opposite: *generous*

meaning (n)

intention, significance, sense
What is the **meaning** of this word?

medium (adj)

middle-sized, normal, standard, average
I'd like a **medium** coffee please.

meet (v)

1. encounter, bump into, see
I like to **meet** my cousin at the park.

2. join, connect, merge
The rivers **meet** below the hill.

3. gather, assemble
The team will **meet** at the entrance.

meeting (n)

gathering, conference, get-together
The teachers are having a **meeting**
about the school disco.

mend (v)

fix, repair, patch up, restore
I asked my sister to **mend** my toy plane.
opposite: *break*

mess (n)

jumble, muddle, clutter, shambles, tip
Look at the **mess** in your bedroom!

messy (adj)

disorganized, untidy, muddled
Charlie's hair is always **messy**.
opposite: *tidy*

might (n)

power, strength, force
The superhero had the **might**
of ten men.

might (v)

could
We **might** go to the pool later.

mild (adj)

1. warm, pleasant
The weather is **mild** for November.

2. meek, calm, easy-going, gentle
He is a **mild** man and never shouts.

mind (v)

1. object, be upset, disapprove
Do you **mind** if I play with your ball?

2. look after, keep an eye on, guard,
watch over
I will **mind** your bag for you.

miserable (adj)

unhappy, desolate, glum, downcast,
sad, downhearted
Mason was **miserable** because he had
lost his dog in the park.
opposite: *cheerful*

mist (n)

fog, haze, drizzle, cloud
I couldn't see very far ahead
because of the **mist**.

mistake (n)

error, slip-up, blunder
Olivia made lots of **mistakes** in
the maths test.

mix (v)

1. blend, combine
Mix the flour and butter together.

2. confuse, jumble, muddle
Don't **mix** up the blue balls and the
red balls.

a
b
c
d
e
f
g
h
i
j
k
l
m
n
o
p
q
r
s
t
u
v
w
x
y
z

a
b
c
d
e
f
g
h
i
j
k
l
m
n
o
p
q
r
s
t
u
v
w
x
y
z

moan (v)

1. groan, whine, howl
The wind **moaned** all night long.

2. grumble, complain, fuss, whinge, whine
Don't **moan** about the weather.

mock (v)

tease, jeer at, make fun of, ridicule
Don't **mock** Alice, just because she is new.

mock (adj)

fake, imitation, pretend, artificial
Max's jacket is made of **mock** leather.
opposite: *genuine, real*

modern (adj)

up-to-date, trendy, current
Ahmed's school is in a **modern** building with all the latest facilities.
opposite: *old-fashioned*

moment (n)

minute, few seconds, instant, short time
Wait a **moment** while I fetch my coat.

money (n)

1. cash, change, dosh, coins
Do you have **money** to buy sweets?

2. savings, riches, earnings
Dad has made lots of **money** over the years.

monster (n)

beast, creature, ogre
There is a scary **monster** under the bridge.

mood (n)

temper, humour, state of mind
My mum is in a bad **mood** today.

more

extra, additional, further
Please may I have some **more** food?
opposite: *less, fewer*

mostly

largely, chiefly, usually, principally, in general, generally, mainly
They are **mostly** older children who go to choir practice.

mouldy (adj)

rotten, decayed
The bread went **mouldy** while we were away.

mound (n)

pile, mountain, heap, hill
There was a **mound** of sand where the mole had been digging.

move (v)

See page 127

movement (n)

motion, action, activity
The police officer watched the house for any sign of **movement**.
See also page 124

moving (adj)

emotional, stirring, touching
Yesterday I watched a very **moving** film which made me cry.

mud (n)

dirt, soil, muck, filth
When my dog climbed out of the river, he was covered with **mud**.

muddle (n)

mess, mix-up, confusion, jumble
My socks are all in a **muddle**.

must (v)

1. has to, should, is compelled to, is obliged to
Kate **must** put on a coat before going out.
2. is bound to be, is surely, has to be, is probably
It **must** be dark by now.

a
b
c
d
e
f
g
h
i
j
k
l
m
n
o
p
q
r
s
t
u
v
w
x
y
z

Nn

nag (v)

pester, bother, hassle, ask, demand
Don't **nag** me to work all the time.

naked (adj)

nude, unclothed, undressed, bare
The boy was **naked** when he had
a shower.

nap (n)

snooze, short sleep, forty winks, rest,
lie-down
Granddad had a **nap** after lunch.

narrow (adj)

thin, slender, close
There is only a **narrow** gap to
squeeze through.
opposite: *wide*

nasty (adj)

1. unpleasant, disgusting, foul, vile,
repulsive, gross, terrible, sickening
There is a **nasty** smell coming from
the drains.
opposite: *pleasant*

2. unkind, cruel, harsh, unpleasant,
unfriendly, spiteful, mean, horrid
The **nasty** teacher shouted at the
children all the time.

3. ugly, unpleasant, messy, horrible
We need to put a bandage on that
nasty cut.

naughty (adj)

disobedient, badly behaved,
mischievous, troublesome
The **naughty** puppy chewed up
a slipper.

near

close to, by, beside, next to
I live **near** the sea, so I have been
able to swim since I was tiny.
opposite: *far from*

nearly

almost, approaching, close to
Go to bed! It's **nearly** midnight.

neat (adj)

1. tidy, smart
She looked **neat** in her new uniform.
opposite: *untidy*

2. uncluttered, organized, arranged, orderly
I have to make sure my room is **neat** for when my cousin comes to stay.
opposite: *disordered*

need (v)

1. require, demand, want
The explorers **need** boots to wade through the water.

2. rely on, depend on, must have
My great-grandparents **need** help to get upstairs.

3. must, have to, are compelled to, ought to, should
We **need** to buy a present before Ella's birthday party.

nervous (adj)

anxious, worried, on edge, scared, frightened, fearful, tense, concerned, jittery, tense, jumpy
The boy was **nervous** when he went to hospital.
opposite: *confident*

new (adj)

1. fresh, clean, unused
Start each exercise on a **new** page.

2. modern, recently built, just bought
They are building a **new** house at the edge of my village.
opposite: *old*

3. novel, original, up-to-date, the latest
This is a **new** style of computer.

4. extra, additional, unknown, unfamiliar
The explorer found two **new** types of crocodile.

nice (adj)

See page 127

noise (n)

sound, din, racket, uproar
Stop making that terrible **noise**!

noisy (adj)

loud, blaring, deafening
That music is far too **noisy**!
opposite: *quiet*

normal (adj)

usual, regular, average, ordinary, standard
I was tired all day, even though I'd had a **normal** amount of sleep.
opposite: *abnormal*

a
b
c
d
e
f
g
h
i
j
k
l
m
n
o
p
q
r
s
t
u
v
w
x
y
z

nosy (adj)

curious, inquisitive, intrusive, snooping, prying
My **nosy** neighbour is always looking over the fence.

note (n)

message, letter
James secretly passed a **note** to Harry during the maths lesson.

notice (n)

1. poster, sign
There is a **notice** about a lost dog on that tree.

2. pay no attention to, ignore, take no heed of
Take no notice of my brother – he is being silly.

notice (v)

spot, see, observe, detect, become aware of
Did you **notice** the tiger in the playground?

now

1. straight away, this moment, without delay, immediately, instantly
Please get in the car – we are going to the shops **now**.
opposite: *later*

2. at the moment, these days, currently, at present
They **now** have three dogs.

3. so far, up to the present
We have **now** lived in this flat for six years.

number (n)

1. figure, digit
Which **number** comes after seven in this sequence?

2. quantity, amount
I could eat any **number** of cakes!

Oo

object (n)

thing, item, article
There are six **objects** on the tray.

odd (adj)

1. strange, weird, bizarre, unusual, out of the ordinary, extraordinary, funny, peculiar
The man down the road is very **odd**.

2. unmatched, mismatched, different
Emma is wearing **odd** socks.

often

frequently, regularly
The cat is **often** shut out all night.
opposite: *seldom*

old (adj)

1. elderly, aged
The **old** woman walks her dog past here.
opposite: *young*

2. shabby, well-used, worn-out, tattered, ragged, battered
It's better to wear **old** clothes to clear the pond.
opposite: *new*

3. ancient, historic, early, antique
We went to an **old** castle on a school trip.
opposite: *modern*

once

1. one time
I've been to France **once**.

2. when, after, following
Once Eliza has put her shoes on, she can go out.

3. previously, formerly, in the past, long ago
There was **once** a grumpy old wizard.

only (adj)

sole, single, solitary, last
That is the **only** piece of chocolate cake left.

a
b
c
d
e
f
g
h
i
j
k
l
m
n
o
p
q
r
s
t
u
v
w
x
y
z

a
b
c
d
e
f
g
h
i
j
k
l
m
n
o
p
q
r
s
t
u
v
w
x
y
z

open (v)

1. unfasten, undo
Open the window – it's hot in here.
opposite: *close*

2. unwrap, undo, untie
We will **open** our Christmas presents after dinner.

3. start, begin, commence, kick off, launch
The school fair will **open** at 3 o'clock this afternoon.
opposite: *end, finish*

open (adj)

1. undone, unfastened, ajar, wide, gaping
When the door is **open**, the mice come inside.
opposite: *shut*

2. trading
When the shop is **open**, we can buy more milk.
opposite: *closed*

3. honest, frank
She was **open** about her fear of cats.
opposite: *secretive*

opening (n)

1. gap, hole, crack, passage, breach, split
A weasel can creep through a small **opening**.

2. launch, premiere
The actor wore a red dress to the **opening** of the film.

3. start, beginning, introduction
The **opening** of that piece of music is very loud.
opposite: *ending, close*

ordinary (adj)

normal, average, mundane, unremarkable, standard, routine, typical, regular, everyday
He said he was a very **ordinary** man, yet he kept four pet leopards.
opposite: *extraordinary*

organize (v)

1. arrange, plan, sort out, set up
We will **organize** a party next month.

2. order, sort out, classify
Organize the children's shirts by colour, please.

original (adj)

1. authentic, genuine, real, actual
Is that the **original** painting or a copy?

2. first, earliest, initial, native
The **original** Native Americans lived in tents made from animal skins.

ornament (n)

decoration, knick-knack
My granny has a row of **ornaments** on the windowsill.

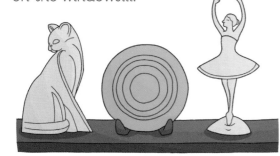

other (adj)

1. different, opposite
We need to find a bridge to get to the **other** side of the river.

2. alternative, different
There are **other** shops if that one is closed.

outside (n)

exterior, shell, face, façade
The **outside** of the egg is speckled.

outside

outdoors
The sun is shining, so let's have lunch **outside**.

overtake (v)

go past, pass, outstrip
My dad drives slowly so all the cars **overtake** us.

own (v)

1. possess, have
I **own** four colouring books.

2. confess, admit
Katie **owned up** to being a bully.

own (adj)

personal
I have always wanted my **own** pony.

own

alone, by oneself, independently
I went **on my own** to the supermarket.

a
b
c
d
e
f
g
h
i
j
k
l
m
n
o
p
q
r
s
t
u
v
w
x
y
z

a
b
c
d
e
f
g
h
i
j
k
l
m
n
o
p
q
r
s
t
u
v
w
x
y
z

Pp

pack (n)

1. bag, luggage
The traveller strapped his **pack** on to the donkey's back.

2. packet, box, package, carton
Tilly bought a **pack** of twelve crayons.

pack (v)

1. fill, load
You need to **pack** your bag before going away.

2. cram, crowd, squeeze, stuff, fit
The elves had to **pack** all the toys into one big sack.

3. put in, stow
Don't forget to **pack** your toothbrush!

pain (n)

1. agony, torment, anguish
The sailor was in great **pain** because he had slipped and banged his head.

2. ache, twinge, hurt
Theo has a slight **pain** in his arm.

3. nuisance, annoyance, trouble
My sister is such a **pain** – she's always singing loudly.

pan (n)

saucepan, frying pan, wok
Tip the chopped onions into the **pan**.

panic (n)

alarm, fright, hysteria, terror, fear
Helen felt a wave of **panic** when she saw the crocodile.
opposite: *calm*

parade (n)

march, procession, troop
The **parade** was exciting to watch.

parcel (n)

package, packet, present
The postman delivered a large **parcel** on my birthday.

part (n)

1. portion, piece, slice, section, segment, fraction, share
My friend gave me a **part** of his pizza.
opposite: *all*

2. role, character
Luke had the main **part** in the play.

3. area, region, district
The swimming pool is in the furthest **part** of town.

particularly

especially, very, extremely, unusually, exceptionally
The painting is not **particularly** valuable.

party (n)

celebration, get-together, ball, dance, festivity, jolly, knees-up, bash
We will have a **party** to welcome my sister home.

past (n)

history, times gone by, earlier times
In the **past**, there were no cars.

patch (n)

area, space, place
There is a small vegetable **patch** in our garden.

patch (v)

fix, repair, mend, cover
The captain needs to **patch** the hole in his boat.

path (n)

alley, pathway, track, footpath, trail, passage, passageway
Rachel followed the **path** to the river.

patient (adj)

tolerant, calm, easy-going, unhurried
Jo was **patient** with the new puppy.

pause (n)

gap, interval, break, rest
There will be a **pause** in the activity when you can get a drink.

pause (v)

stop, take a break, hesitate, halt
Let's **pause** so I can read the sign.

pay (n)

wages, salary, income, earnings
Dad receives his **pay** every Thursday.

pay (v)

1. spend, hand over
How much did you **pay** for that?

2. settle, clear
Who will **pay** the restaurant bill?

a
b
c
d
e
f
g
h
i
j
k
l
m
n
o
p
q
r
s
t
u
v
w
x
y
z

a
b
c
d
e
f
g
h
i
j
k
l
m
n
o
p
q
r
s
t
u
v
w
x
y
z

people (n)

1. persons, individuals, folk
There are lots of **people** at the football match.

2. citizens, nationals, population, community
The **people** of Germany enjoy a good standard of living.

3. humans, human beings
People have been on Earth for fewer than a million years.

perfect (adj)

ideal, exactly right, spot on, faultless, flawless
Betty gave me the **perfect** present.

person (n)

individual, human being
Choose a **person** to be your partner for the game.

personality (n)

character, features, traits, nature
The scientist has a very difficult **personality**.

phone (n)

telephone, mobile, cell phone, smartphone
Can I borrow your **phone** to make a call?

phone (v)

call, ring, telephone
Don't forget to **phone** Lucy later.

photograph (n)

photo, image, snap, picture
Do you have a **photograph** of your dog?

pick (n)

choice, selection
Take your **pick** of the biscuits.

pick (v)

1. choose, select, decide on
You can **pick** a film to see on your birthday.

2. gather, collect, harvest, pluck
Rebecca went to **pick** strawberries in the garden.

pick up (v)

1. retrieve, collect, fetch
We will **pick up** the parcel from the post office later.

2. lift, raise
Please **pick up** the baby – she's crying.

picture (n)

illustration, painting, drawing, artwork, piece of art, cartoon
Anita drew a beautiful **picture** in the art room.

piece (n)

1. slice, chunk, slab, portion, lump
Eddie had a **piece** of pie and some custard.

2. scrap, sheet, leaf
Take a **piece** of paper and write down your name.

pile (n)

heap, mound, mass, stack, bundle, mountain
I left a **pile** of dirty washing in my room.

pile (v)

heap, stack
We had to **pile** the books upstairs when the front room flooded.

pillar (n)

column
The traveller tied his horse to a **pillar** outside the temple.

pity (n)

1. compassion, sympathy, concern
The monk showed **pity** to the poor, sick people.

2. shame, source of sorrow, sad fact
It is a **pity** that your friends have moved away.

pity (v)

sympathize with, feel sorry for
I **pity** you having to live next door to that noisy dog.

place (n)

1. position, location, site, venue, spot
The park is a good **place** to learn to cycle.

2. seat, slot, space, opening
There is one more **place** left on the school trip.

place (v)

position, leave, put, deposit, arrange, set down
Can you **place** the hamster cage by the window, please?

a
b
c
d
e
f
g
h
i
j
k
l
m
n
o
p
q
r
s
t
u
v
w
x
y
z

plain

a
b
c
d
e
f
g
h
i
j
k
l
m
n
o
p
q
r
s
t
u
v
w
x
y
z

plain (adj)

1. obvious, clear, apparent, noticeable
It is **plain** that you are not interested in this subject.

2. simple, unadorned, unflavoured, unscented, undecorated
Jo bought two striped T-shirts and a **plain** one.

3. simple, unadorned, dull, frugal, ordinary
The room was very **plain**, with just a chair and a rug.

plan (n)

1. proposal, suggestion, idea, strategy, plot
We had a **plan** for the day, but when it rained we had to think again.

2. draft, drawing, design
The man showed us the **plans** for a new swimming pool.

plan (v)

aim, plot, propose, intend
We **plan** to escape in a hot-air balloon.

play (n)

performance, drama, production, show
Harry went to see a **play** at the local theatre.

play (v)

1. amuse oneself, have fun, entertain oneself
The children can **play** until teatime.

2. perform
The band will **play** at the concert hall on Friday.

3. compete against, tackle, challenge, oppose
Whenever we **play** that team we win!

playful (adj)

lively, mischievous, bouncy, spirited
Harriet has a **playful** puppy and a lazy older dog.

plead (v)

beg, implore
No matter how much you **plead** with me, you're not going to that party.

pleasant (adj)

1. pleasing, enjoyable, fine
We spent a **pleasant** day in the countryside.
opposite: *unpleasant*

2. friendly, good-natured, kind
The nurse was **pleasant**, and chatted to me for ages.

plenty

enough, sufficient, lots of, ample
We have **plenty of** cake to go round.

plot (n)

1. plan, scheme, conspiracy
The aliens came up with a **plot** to hide their spaceship in the shed.

2. storyline, sequence of events, narrative, what happened
I thought the film was boring because I couldn't follow the **plot**.

plump (adj)

fat, dumpy, overweight, large
My cat is so **plump** she can't fit through the cat flap.

poison (n)

venom, toxin
The witch used **poison** to kill the dwarf.

poke (v)

1. prod, push at, jab
The naughty boys **poke** the worms with sticks to see if they will move.

2. stick out, protrude, thrust
The crocuses **poke** through the snow in January.

polite (adj)

courteous, well-mannered, gracious
Lola is always **polite**, even when she's feeling tired.
opposite: *rude*

poor (adj)

1. poverty-stricken, destitute, badly off, hard up
That family is so **poor** they can't afford shoes.
opposite: *rich*

2. unfortunate, unlucky, wretched
The **poor** cats were left without food for three days.

3. low-quality, inferior, shoddy, below standard, unsatisfactory
The food is very **poor** in that new pizza place.
opposite: *good*

a b c d e f g h i j k l m n o p q r s t u v w x y z

pop

pop (n)
bang, explosion
The balloon burst with a **pop**.

pop (v)
1. burst, break
Please don't **pop** the bubbles
I am blowing.

2. stop by, call in, visit
Please will you **pop in** to see
Grandma on your way home?

popular (adj)
well-liked, favoured, well-received
The book about aliens was
very **popular**.

pour (v)
gush, cascade, run
Did you see the water **pour** through
the hole in the roof?

power (n)
1. authority, right
The king had the **power** to choose
which knights went to battle.

2. energy, electricity
There was enough **power** left in the
camera to take a few photos.

3. strength, might, ability, force
The alien had the **power** of ten
warriors.

present (n)
gift
Oscar gave his friend a **present** but
didn't stay for the party.

present (v)
1. award, hand over, give
The mayor will **present** Liam with
a medal for bravery.

2. display, show, demonstrate
Karen will **present** her project to
the class.

present (adj)
in attendance, around, here, there
An adult must be **present** at
all times.

press (v)
1. push, depress, hit
Press the button to call the attendant.

2. put pressure on, persuade,
urge, encourage
The market sellers **press** my mum to
buy things she doesn't want.

3. squeeze, push, compress, squish
Press the dough into a loaf shape.

pretend (v)
act as, pose as
I will **pretend to be** the genie, and you can be Aladdin.

pretend (adj)
make-believe, made-up, fake, fictional, artificial
The pirate had a **pretend** scar on his face.

pretty (adj)
lovely, attractive, beautiful, gorgeous, stunning, good-looking, handsome
Granny lives in a **pretty** cottage with flowers around the door.

pretty
fairly, quite, rather, somewhat
The ogre is **pretty** lazy and sleeps all day.

price (n)
cost, charge
What is the **price** of that football?

probable (adj)
likely, expected, most plausible
The **probable** cause of the rumbling sound was a yeti rolling down the mountain.
opposite: *unlikely*

probably
likely
The dragon will **probably** choke if he eats a knight in full armour.

promise (n)
pledge, oath, commitment, vow
I made a **promise** to wear the friendship bracelet forever.

promise (v)
swear, give your word, vow
Do you **promise** to tell me if you see anyone coming?

proper (adj)
1. right, correct, appropriate, suitable
Is that the **proper** hammer for fossil-hunting?
2. prim, decent, respectable
Lizzie is very **proper** and has good manners.

properly
correctly, fully, suitably
Turn the handle **properly** or the door won't open.

protect (v)
guard, watch over, safeguard
The gamekeepers **protect** rhinos and elephants from poachers.

a
b
c
d
e
f
g
h
i
j
k
l
m
n
o
p
q
r
s
t
u
v
w
x
y
z

a
b
c
d
e
f
g
h
i
j
k
l
m
n
o
p
q
r
s
t
u
v
w
x
y
z

pudding (n)

dessert, sweet, afters
What would you like for **pudding**?

puff (n)

cloud, burst, whiff
The dragon let out a **puff** of smoke when he sneezed.

puff (v)

1. wheeze, pant, gasp, huff
The giant **puffed** as he climbed the steep hill.

2. blow, waft
The old wizard likes to **puff** clouds of blue smoke from his pipe.

pull (v)

1. haul, drag, tug, draw, tow, heave
Two horses could barely **pull** the chariot up the hill.

2. remove, extract
The dentist had to **pull out** four of my teeth.

3. withdraw from, drop out of, retire from
Chris had to **pull out of** the race because he broke his ankle.

punch (v)

thump, strike, hit
The goblin **punched** the giant, but the giant didn't notice.

push (v)

1. force, shove, press, thrust, barge
You will have to **push** your way to the front of the crowd if you want to see more clearly.

2. encourage, pressure, urge, pressurize
Chris's mum **pushed** him to try ballet, but he preferred gym.

3. force, squeeze, press, cram, pack, squash
Fran had to **push** everything into one box so it would fit in the car.

put (v)

See page 127

put away (v)
tidy up, tidy away, store
Put away your toys and go to bed.

put off (v)
delay, defer, postpone
Isla **put off** hanging out the washing because it was raining.

put out (adj)
offended, upset, hurt, annoyed
Jacob was **put out** that he had not been invited to the party.

put right (v)
correct, make amends for, fix
If you **put right** all the things you did wrong, you can have a second chance.

put together (v)
make, construct, build
Put together your model aeroplane tomorrow.

put up (v)
raise, lift, show
Put up your hand if you can swim.

put up with (v)
suffer, endure, tolerate
He had to **put up with** his aunt all weekend.

Qq

quality (n)
grade, standard, class
The cheese is of a very high **quality**.

quantity (n)
amount, number
My uncle has collected a large **quantity** of old computer parts.

quest (n)
expedition, hunt, adventure, mission
The knight went on a **quest** to find the dragon.

question (n)
query, enquiry, puzzle, problem
I want to ask a **question**.

a
b
c
d
e
f
g
h
i
j
k
l
m
n
o
p
q
r
s
t
u
v
w
x
y
z

a
b
c
d
e
f
g
h
i
j
k
l
m
n
o
p
q
r
s
t
u
v
w
x
y
z

question (v)

interrogate, quiz, ask
The agents **question** the spy about the secret tape.

queue (n)

line, line of people, column of people
There is a long **queue** outside the cinema.

quick (adj)

1. rapid, fast, speedy, nippy, agile
The **quick** brown fox ran across the street.
opposite: *slow*

2. smart, clever, bright, intelligent
Anna is very **quick** – she's good at all subjects.
opposite: *stupid, slow*

3. brief, short
Mum decided to make a **quick** visit to the shops.
opposite: *long*

quickly

rapidly, swiftly, hurriedly, speedily
The hero **quickly** cut off the troll's head, then ran off.

quiet (adj)

peaceful, silent, undisturbed, restful, empty
We sat in a **quiet** place and thought about the soldiers killed in the war.
opposite: *noisy, busy*

quit (v)

give up, stop
My uncle says he is going to quit his job and go travelling.

quite

1. rather, reasonably, fairly
It is **quite** a long way to Japan.

2. completely, entirely, totally, utterly
My two kittens look **quite** different from each other.

quiz (n)

questionnaire, competition, test
We all did a **quiz** on dolphins and whales.

Rr

raise (v)

1. lift, hold up
We had to **raise** our hands above our heads.

2. bring up, nurture, parent
The wild boy was **raised** by wolves.

3. collect, gather, bring in
Our sponsored haircut **raised** lots of money for charity.

range (n)

1. variety, choice, selection, assortment
There is a **range** of different games to cover all interests.

2. spread, band, group
The age **range** for this book is five to eight years.

range (v)

1. wander, roam, rove
The lions **range** over the plains looking for antelope to hunt.

2. span, vary, extend
The hats **range** from tiny sizes for babies to large sizes for adults.

rapid (adj)

fast, quick, speedy, hurried
There was a **rapid** burst of gunfire as the bandits suddenly appeared.
opposite: *slow*

rare (adj)

unusual, scarce, uncommon
The **rare** bird lives on only one island.
opposite: *common*

rarely

infrequently, scarcely, seldom
It **rarely** snows in the summer.
opposite: *often*

rate (n)

1. speed, pace
Zach can recite his times tables at an amazing **rate**.

2. frequency
The crime **rate** is low in my village.

3. charge, fee, cost, price
They charge a very high **rate** to advertise on television.

a b c d e f g h i j k l m n o p q r s t u v w x y z

a
b
c
d
e
f
g
h
i
j
k
l
m
n
o
p
q
r
s
t
u
v
w
x
y
z

rather (adj)

quite, a bit, fairly, moderately, somewhat
It is **rather** cold today.

rather

sooner, prefer to
I would **rather** go swimming than go to the park.

raw (adj)

uncooked
Sushi is made from **raw** fish.
opposite: *cooked*

ray (n)

beam, shaft
A **ray** of sunlight turned the vampire to dust.

reach (v)

1. touch, get, pick up
Can you **reach** the book on that high shelf?

2. arrive at, come to
We will **reach** the coast by teatime.

3. attain, arrive at
I hope I will **reach** my target for my sponsored swim.

4. stretch, extend, hold out
An octopus can **reach** out its tentacles to catch a fish.

ready (adj)

1. prepared, set
Are you **ready** to go out?

2. done, completed, prepared
The dinner is **ready**.

real (adj)

1. genuine, authentic, actual
There is a **real** genie in that lamp.

2. true, honest, genuine, sincere
The prince had a **real** love for the mermaid.

realistic (adj)

1. lifelike, convincing
We made a **realistic** model of a bird.

2. reasonable, practical, sensible
Do you have a **realistic** idea of when you'll be ready?

really

1. extremely, very, exceptionally
We had a **really** tasty meal on my mum's birthday.

2. genuinely, actually, truly, honestly
Did Alice **really** find a fairy in her garden?

record (n)

note, account, list, log
We made a **record** of how many cars, buses and bikes went past in one hour.

record (v)

tape, video, film, make a recording of
Mr Graham will **record** the concert
and put it on the school website.

recover (v)

1. get better, recuperate, improve,
rally, heal
Gaby has **recovered** from the cold
she had last week.

2. bring back, rescue, restore, retrieve
The expedition has **recovered** a
shipwreck from the seabed.

regular (adj)

1. standard, normal, ordinary,
average, medium
Dad ordered a **regular** coffee and a
large cake.

2. evenly spaced, frequent, fixed
The buses come at **regular** intervals.

relax (v)

1. rest, unwind, chill, hang out
After school, I like to **relax** by
playing games.
opposite: *work*

2. loosen, ease, slacken
Relax your muscles and it will
hurt less.
opposite: *tense, tighten*

relaxed (adj)

casual, carefree, easy-going,
leisurely, laid-back
My mum is very **relaxed** – she lets
us go to bed when we want.

rely on (v)

depend on, count on, trust, bank on
We can always **rely on** Robbie to
bring enough snacks for everyone.

remain (v)

1. stay, wait
One alien will **remain** on board while
the others explore the new planet.

2. are left, survive
Only a few sticks **remained** of the
tree house.

3. stay, continue, carry on
It will **remain** hot all weekend.

a
b
c
d
e
f
g
h
i
j
k
l
m
n
o
p
q
r
s
t
u
v
w
x
y
z

remains (n)

1. leftovers, scraps, leavings
The old gentleman fed the **remains** of the feast to the dogs.

2. body, corpse, carcass
The scientist took the **remains** of the tiger to the lab.

remember (v)

recall, recollect
Do you **remember** the day we went skating?
opposite: *forget*

remove (v)

1. take off
Remove your shoes before entering.

2. delete, take away, cut off, erase
We decided to **remove** a strip from the left of the picture.

3. take out, dismiss, send away
You will be **removed** from class if you keep shouting.

repeat (v)

1. copy, reproduce, say again
Repeat what I say carefully.

2. redo, do again, do over
You will have to **repeat** that exercise if you don't do it properly.

3. recite
Louise can **repeat** the poem from memory.

replace (v)

1. change, renew
We need to **replace** our computer as it is too old and slow.

2. take over from, follow
Troy will **replace** Joe as book monitor.

3. put back, return, restore
Annabelle **replaced** the trumpet she had played.

reply (v)

answer, respond
You must **reply** if the police officer asks you a question.

report (n)

account (of), description (of)
Write a **report** on the experiment you did yesterday.

report (v)

1. check in, go, present yourself
You have to **report** to the front desk when you arrive.

2. inform on, tell on, complain about
The dinner ladies will **report** you to the teachers if you cause trouble.

3. give an account of, record, describe, write about
The school magazine **reported on** the summer fair.

require (v)

1. need, demand, instruct
Mrs Ahmed **requires** us to arrive early.

2. must, have to, need to
We are **required** to take waterproof clothes on our trip.

rescue (v)

save, free, liberate, release
The hero will **rescue** the stranded boy.

responsible (adj)

1. reliable, dependable, trustworthy
Libby is very **responsible**; she can look after your dog while you are away.

2. to blame, guilty (of)
Who is **responsible** for breaking this window?

3. in charge of
Maya is **responsible for** handing out the book bags.

rest (n)

1. break, pause, breather
Have a short **rest** and then we will go for a run.

2. relaxation, time off, quiet time
You need **rest** when you are ill.

3. remaining, other
Where are the **rest** of the biscuits?

rest (v)

relax, recuperate, take a break, chill out
The warriors must **rest** before they go into battle.

restaurant (n)

café, snack bar, canteen, eatery coffee shop, bistro
We always have dinner in a **restaurant** on my birthday.

restless (adj)

anxious, agitated, jumpy, jittery, nervous, on edge
The children were **restless** because it was the last day of term.

result (n)

1. outcome, findings, verdict, upshot
What was the **result** of your test?

2. score, outcome
The **result** of the match was 4-0.

a
b
c
d
e
f
g
h
i
j
k
l
m
n
o
p
q
r
s
t
u
v
w
x
y
z

a
b
c
d
e
f
g
h
i
j
k
l
m
n
o
p
q
r
s
t
u
v
w
x
y
z

result (v)

bring about, cause, produce
The fire **resulted in** massive damage
to the hall.

return (v)

1. bring back, restore
Karl will **return** your football
tomorrow.

2. revisit, go back
We will **return** to that beach
next year.

3. get back, come home, arrive back,
When will Dad **return**?

revolting (adj)

disgusting, foul, vile, horrid,
appalling, repulsive, repellent
The troll ate a **revolting** mixture
of toads, goats and mud.

reward (n)

prize, payment
The old lady offered a **reward**
for the return of her cat.

reward (v)

1. commend, honour
The King will **reward** the soldier for
his bravery.

2. pay
If you carry this message, I will
reward you handsomely.

rich (adj)

wealthy, well-off, prosperous,
affluent
The prince was so **rich** he could
afford three castles.

ride (n)

cycle, trip, journey, spin
Greg wants to go for a **ride** on
his bike.

right (n)

freedom, power, authority
My brother doesn't have the **right**
to tell me what to do.

right (adj)

correct, accurate, spot on
Work out the sum carefully so you
get the **right** answer.
opposite: *wrong*

ripe (adj)

ready, fully grown, mature
The pears are **ripe** early this year.
opposite: *unripe*

rise (v)

1. come up, appear
The sun will **rise** in a couple of hours.
opposite: *set*

2. go up, ascend, float, soar
Watch the hot-air balloon **rise** into the sky.
opposite: *drop, fall*

3. increase, shoot up, go up
Prices **rise** every year.
opposite: *decrease, drop*

river (n)

stream, brook, canal, burn
The **river** flows right past our house.

road (n)

street, path, avenue, highway, lane, track, motorway
This **road** always has lots of traffic.

rob (v)

burgle, steal from, loot, raid
The gang will **rob** the bank.

robbery (n)

burglary, theft, mugging
The police investigated the **robbery**.

rod (n)

1. stick, pole
Dad used a long **rod** to get my football off the roof.

2. bar, strut, support
There are steel **rods** inside the concrete to make the bridge strong.

role (n)

part, character
My aunt played the **role** of the fairy godmother in the pantomime.

roll (v)

1. tumble, turn over and over
It is fun to **roll** down a grassy hill.

2. flatten, smooth
Roll out the pastry for the pie.

a
b
c
d
e
f
g
h
i
j
k
l
m
n
o
p
q
r
s
t
u
v
w
x
y
z

room (n)

1. hall, chamber
The witch led the goblin into a spooky **room**.

2. space
Is there **room** for me in the car?

rope (n)

cord, line, cable
They tied the dog to the tree with a **rope**.

rotten (adj)

decayed, rancid, spoiled
Those vegetables are **rotten**.

rough (adj)

1. uneven, bumpy, lumpy, scratchy
A shark has **rough** skin.
opposite: *smooth*

2. stormy, choppy
The boat sailed through **rough** seas.
opposite: *calm*

3. quick, crude, hasty
Elizabeth made a **rough** sketch of the dress she wanted to make.
opposite: *careful, detailed*

4. harsh, hard, cruel, brusque
The ogre gave the gnome **rough** treatment.
opposite: *kind, gentle*

round (adj)

1. circular, ring-shaped
Ed's bedroom has a **round** window.

2. spherical, ball-shaped
Oranges and grapefruit are **round** fruit.

row (n)

1. (rhymes with 'go') line, column
Stand in a **row** so I can count you.

2. (rhymes with 'cow') argument, fight, squabble, disagreement
Ali had a **row** with his sister.

3. (rhymes with 'cow') noise, din, racket, commotion
Do you have to make such a **row** with that drum kit?

rub (v)

1. spread, smear
Rub this cream on the wasp sting.

2. polish, buff
Rub the lamp and a genie will appear.

3. erase, remove
Rub out the mistakes in your homework.

rubbish (n)
garbage, trash, litter, refuse, waste, junk
We put all the **rubbish** in the bin.

rude (adj)
impolite, offensive, insolent, cheeky
My sister is crying because the new boy was **rude** to her.

ruin (v)
spoil, destroy, damage, wreck
The rain will **ruin** your velvet jacket.

ruins (n)
remains
The ghost haunts the **ruins** on the hill.

rule (n)
law, restriction, regulation
There is a **rule** that says you must not run in the corridor.

rule (v)
govern, reign, have control
The emperor hoped to **rule** for fifty years.

run (n)
jog, sprint
I'm planning to go for a **run** before I play cricket.

run (v)
1. dash, hurry, sprint, rush
Run for the bus, or you'll miss it!

2. operate, work
Today's cars **run** on unleaded petrol.

3. control, organize, operate, be in charge of
My friend will **run** the tombola at the school fair.

4. flow, trickle, pour, gush, dribble, fall
The water will **run** down the wall when it rains.

runny (adj)
watery, thin, fluid, liquid
This custard is too **runny**.

rush (n)
1. hurry
We are in a **rush** because we didn't leave early enough.

2. crush, stampede
There was a sudden **rush** for the exits when the alarm sounded.

3. flood, gush, torrent, spurt, stream
The dam burst and there was a **rush** of water.

rush (v)
hurry, hasten, make haste, dash, run, speed up
The family will need to **rush** because the plane leaves soon.

a
b
c
d
e
f
g
h
i
j
k
l
m
n
o
p
q
r
s
t
u
v
w
x
y
z

a
b
c
d
e
f
g
h
i
j
k
l
m
n
o
p
q
r
s
t
u
v
w
x
y
z

Ss

sad (adj)

1. unhappy, miserable, depressed, gloomy
The boy was **sad** because he had lost his ball.
opposite: *happy*

2. pitiful, heart-rending, heartbreaking, mournful
They heard a **sad** cry from the tower.

sadness (n)

unhappiness, misery, sorrow, depression, grief
She was overcome with **sadness**.

safe (adj)

1. secure, out of danger, protected, out of harm's way, unharmed
You will be **safe** in here.

2. harmless
This type of snake is **safe** – it will not bite.
opposite: *dangerous*

safety (n)

security, well-being
The teacher considered the children's **safety** when choosing activities.

same (adj)

identical, matching, alike
Emily's sandals and Netta's sandals are the **same** colour.
opposite: *different*

save (v)

1. preserve, conserve, protect
We will have to work hard to **save** the tigers.

2. keep, hold on to, retain
You should **save** your money for something you really want.

3. rescue, recover, retrieve
The farmer tried to **save** her cows from the flood.

say (v)
See page 128

scare (n)

fright, jolt
The ghost gave me a **scare**.

scare (v)

frighten, terrify, shock, alarm, horrify
Ed tried to **scare** us by making a loud noise.

scary (adj)

frightening, alarming, worrying, spooky, eerie, ghostly
There was a **scary** sound downstairs.

score (v)

achieve, gain, win
Our team might still **score** a goal
in the last few minutes.

scrap (n)

1. fragment, shred, piece
He wrote a note on a **scrap** of paper.

2. morsels, waste food, crumbs
My auntie always feeds her dog
scraps of chicken.

3. junk, waste, rubbish
The brothers went from door to
door collecting **scrap**.

scratch (n)

scrape, mark, groove
There is a **scratch** on Dad's car.

scratch (v)

graze, scrape, cut, tear, gouge
Amina **scratched** her
leg on a bramble.

scream (n)

shriek, yell, screech, call, cry,
wail, howl
We heard a blood-curdling **scream**
from the tower.

scruffy (adj)

bedraggled, ragged, battered,
tattered, tatty, rough, shabby,
beaten about, beaten up
The tramp wore a **scruffy** coat
and a torn hat.

sea (n)

1. ocean
Hagfish live deep in the **sea**.

2. coast, seaside
I prefer the **sea** to the countryside.

3. waves, swell
The **sea** is rough today.

search (v)

look, hunt, scout
We went into the wood to **search**
for the lost dog.

seaside (n)

coast, beach, seashore,
coastline, sands
Our day at the **seaside** was
great fun.

a
b
c
d
e
f
g
h
i
j
k
l
m
n
o
p
q
r
s
t
u
v
w
x
y
z

a
b
c
d
e
f
g
h
i
j
k
l
m
n
o
p
q
r
s
t
u
v
w
x
y
z

secret (adj)

1. hidden, concealed
The children crept into a **secret** passageway.

2. confidential, private, restricted
The spy stole the **secret** documents.

see (v)

1. watch, view, look at
Do you want to **see** that film about the polar bear?

2. witness, observe
Did you **see** the firework display?

3. meet, catch up with, encounter, bump into
I will **see** you in the playground later.

4. report to, visit, call on
You'll have to **see** the head teacher about your behaviour.

seem (v)

appear
It doesn't **seem** to be raining any longer.

send (v)

1. dispatch, post, mail, email, text
I will **send** my older brother a message.

2. pack off
I will **send** you home if you don't behave.

sensible (adj)

reasonable, practical, rational
Ramiz is a **sensible** boy, so he won't do anything dangerous.
opposite: *silly*

separate (v)

part, split up, divide, take apart
The man had to **separate** the two dogs that were fighting in the park.

separate (adj)

individual, different
The twins always have **separate** birthday cakes.

set (n)

1. collection, batch, group, pack
I have a **set** of model dinosaurs.

2. class, group, band
I have been put in **set** 4B.

set (v)

1. place, position, put
Please **set** the cake down here.

2. harden, go stiff, solidify, go hard
The teacher says my clay model will **set** by tomorrow.

3. arrange, settle on, fix, choose
We have **set** a date for sports day.

4. depart, leave, get going, start
Mum will **set off** on her trip today.

setting (n)

location, position
The **setting** for our play is a desert in America.

shade (n)

1. screen, canopy, parasol
We used a **shade** to keep the picnic food cool.

2. shadow
Alex lay in the **shade** to avoid sunburn.

shade (v)

shield, protect, screen
Shade your eyes when you go outside.

shake (v)

1. tremble, shiver, shudder, quiver, quake
The tiny birds **shake** when the cat comes near.

2. wobble, quiver, sway, vibrate
The jelly **shakes** on the plate.

3. agitate
Pour the other ingredients into the milk and **shake** the mixture.

share (n)

portion, helping, part, ration, allowance
Alexa has eaten my **share**!

share (v)

distribute, hand round, split, divide, divvy up
Share the sweets amongst the class.

sharp (adj)

1. jagged, pointy, cutting
The rocks have **sharp** edges.
opposite: *blunt*

2. bright, clever, intelligent, alert, smart
That boy's **sharp** – he knows what's going on.
opposite: *dim*

3. keen, acute
A hawk has **sharp** eyes to see prey from far away.

4. distinct, clear, marked
There is a **sharp** contrast between Isaac's room and Josh's.

5. stabbing, sudden, violent, fierce, agonizing, shooting
Fatima felt a **sharp** pain in her foot.
opposite: *dull*

shine (v)

gleam, glisten
The floor will **shine** when my dad has polished it.

a
b
c
d
e
f
g
h
i
j
k
l
m
n
o
p
q
r
s
t
u
v
w
x
y
z

a
b
c
d
e
f
g
h
i
j
k
l
m
n
o
p
q
r
s
t
u
v
w
x
y
z

shiny (adj)

bright, gleaming, glistening, glittering, glowing, shining
The queen wore a **shiny** crown and a long cloak.
opposite: *dull*

shock (n)

fright, unpleasant surprise
We had a **shock** when we saw a lion outside the tent.

shock (v)

upset, alarm, dismay, horrify, startle, appal
Dylan likes to **shock** his sisters with scary stories.

shoot (v)

1. fire at, hit
Try to **shoot** the middle of the target.
2. speed, rush, hurry, hurtle, race, whizz
Jamie watched the fire engine **shoot** past on its way to the fire.
opposite: *crawl*

short (adj)

1. small, squat, little, undersized
The gnome was **short** and hairy.
opposite: *tall*
2. brief, fleeting
We only spent a **short** time in the sea, because it was so cold.
opposite: *long*
3. scarce, meagre, limited
Red paint is in **short** supply, so don't use it all.

shout (n)

yell, scream, shriek, call
The villain let out a **shout** as he fell through the ice.

shout (v)

call, yell, cry out
Shout to your brother – he has gone too far ahead.
opposite: *whisper*

show (n)

1. performance, production, play
Rose is going to see a **show** at the theatre with her class.
2. exhibition, display
The art **show** will be open until the weekend.

show (v)

1. present, display
Please **show** me the book you bought.
opposite: *hide*

2. demonstrate, explain, tell, describe, teach
Glen will **show** us how to play chess.

3. lead, guide, conduct, take
The head teacher will **show** the new girl into her classroom.

4. indicate, reveal, demonstrate
This light is here to **show** that someone is using the studio.

5. illustrate, depict, portray, represent
The picture **shows** a bear in a tree.

6. brag, boast, gloat
Harry will probably **show off** about winning a prize.

shrink (v)

reduce, shrivel, grow smaller
Those spots will **shrink** if you put the cream on.
opposite: *grow*

shut (v)

1. close, fasten, lock, secure, slam
Please **shut** the door when you go out.
opposite: *open*

2. locked, imprisoned, confined, put away
The prisoner was **shut** in a tower with rats and mice.

shy (adj)

timid, self-conscious, nervous, bashful, coy, wary
The boy was too **shy** to say his name.

sick (adj)

1. ill, unwell, poorly, off-colour
Emil is **sick** so he can't come to school today.
opposite: *healthy, well*

2. queasy, nauseous
The swell of the sea made the passengers feel **sick**.

side (n)

1. edge, wall, rim
Gracie leaned over the **side** of the boat to see the fish.

2. perimeter, boundary, edge
Anna ran along the **side** of the field.

3. team, squad, party, group
Which **side** do you support?

4. face, façade
The other **side** of the house overlooks the canal.

5. point of view, position
The class had to present both **sides** of the argument.

a
b
c
d
e
f
g
h
i
j
k
l
m
n
o
p
q
r
s
t
u
v
w
x
y
z

sign (n)

1. signal, cue, gesture
The spy made a secret **sign**.

2. trace
There was no **sign** of the lost sheep.

3. poster, notice, information sheet, placard, announcement
There is a **sign** on the wall about what to do if there is a fire.

silence (n)

quiet, stillness, calm
The explosion was followed by **silence**.

silly (adj)

1. funny, humorous, light-hearted, amusing
Zara bought a book of **silly** stories.

2. stupid, idiotic, ridiculous, crazy, ludicrous
Mia's new hat looks **silly**.

simple (adj)

1. plain, straightforward, uncomplicated, modest
We had a **simple** supper because we were too tired to cook.
opposite: *elaborate*

2. plain, easy, clear, understandable, straightforward
The book is written in **simple** language for small children.
opposite: *complicated*

skin (n)

1. leather, hide, pelt, fur
The bag is made of animal **skin**.

2. film, crust
I don't like the **skin** on custard.

slap (v)

smack, spank, swipe, strike, hit, cuff
The evil witch will **slap** the elves if they don't work hard enough.

sleep (n)

snooze, nap, doze, siesta
The old man likes to have a **sleep** in the afternoon.

slice (n)

piece, chunk, portion, share, slab
Arthur has already had a **slice** of tart.

slip (v)

1. slide, glide, slither
With their skates, they **slip** over easily on the ice.

2. trip, fall
Be careful you don't **slip** on the stairs!

slow (adj)

1. unhurried, leisurely, drawn-out
I love having a **slow**, lazy bath.
opposite: *quick*

2. stupid, unintelligent, dense
The boy is rather **slow** – he cannot read properly yet.
opposite: *quick-witted*

3. sluggish, halting
Abi is being **slow** putting on her shoes.
opposite: *fast*

4. dull, uneventful, boring, uninteresting
The tennis this afternoon was **slow**.
opposite: *exciting*

slowly

gradually, bit by bit, lazily
The lion walked **slowly** over the grass.
opposite: *quickly*

small (adj)

little, tiny, titchy
There is a **small** piece of pie left.
opposite: *big*

smart (adj)

1. elegant, tidy, stylish, neat, fashionable
Lottie is wearing a **smart** dress today.
opposite: *shabby*

2. bright, clever, quick, brainy,
Tilly is very **smart** so she'll do well in her exams.
opposite: *dim*

smash (v)

1. break, shatter
Peter **smashed** the window with his cricket ball.

2. crash, bang, bump, collide (with)
The car **smashed** into a wall.

smell (n)

scent, odour, aroma, stench, stink, pong, whiff
There was a strange **smell** in the school laboratory.

a
b
c
d
e
f
g
h
i
j
k
l
m
n
o
p
q
r
s
t
u
v
w
x
y
z

smile (n)

grin, smirk
The boy had a **smile** on his face.

smooth (adj)

1. even, level, flat
The icing is perfectly **smooth**.
opposite: *bumpy*
2. sleek, shiny
The cat has a **smooth** coat.
opposite: *rough*

sneak (v)

creep, prowl, slip, skulk
You have to **sneak** in through the back door.

soft (adj)

1. squashy, squidgy, comfy
Bethany sat in a **soft** chair.
opposite: *hard*
2. mushy, squishy
The bananas have gone **soft**.
opposite: *firm*
3. fluffy, velvety, silky, feathery, downy
My kitten has such **soft** fur.
opposite: *rough*
4. gentle, low, faint, quiet
We could hear **soft** music from upstairs.
opposite: *loud*
5. lenient, kind, tolerant
Luca's parents are too **soft**.
opposite: *strict*

sometimes

occasionally, now and then, from time to time, once in a while
I **sometimes** go to the park on my own.

soon

shortly, briefly, presently, in a little while
It will **soon** be time for bed.

sort (n)

type, kind, variety
Which **sort** of fruit do you like best?

sort (v)

order, organize, arrange, group, categorize

Rajiv needs to **sort** his books by subject.

sound (n)

noise, tone, note

The bat makes a high-pitched **sound**.

sound (adj)

1. solid, secure, steady, safe, reliable

The school is built on **sound** foundations.

opposite: *shaky*

2. reasonable, fair, sensible, rational, good

He had a **sound** reason for leaving his job.

spare (adj)

extra, additional, surplus, standby, backup, in reserve

There is a **spare** tyre in the boot of the car.

spare (v)

1. left over, going free

Is there a bun to **spare**?

2. save, leave

They will kill the rats but **spare** the mice.

sparkle (v)

glitter, gleam, shine

The diamonds in the king's crown **sparkle** in the sunlight.

speak (v)

talk, chat, communicate (with)

Will you **speak** to your brother about joining our team?

special (adj)

1. extraordinary, unusual, remarkable, exceptional, significant

We went on a **special** holiday after I came out of hospital.

opposite: *ordinary*

2. extra, specific, specialized

Zoe needs **special** help with reading.

3. individual, different, personal

Mrs Griggs has a **special** recipe for lemonade.

speed (v)

dash, hurry, hurtle, whizz, race, tear, sweep, zoom

I saw the car **speed** down the hill and round the corner.

opposite: *crawl*

a
b
c
d
e
f
g
h
i
j
k
l
m
n
o
p
q
r
s
t
u
v
w
x
y
z

spill (v)

1. spread, flow, pour, gush, run
Oil can **spill** out of the tankers into the sea.

2. upset, tip out, slop out, slosh
The twins always **spill** their milk at breakfast time.

spin (v)

whirl, twirl, turn, rotate, revolve
The skaters **spin** round on the ice.

spooky (adj)

eerie, scary, frightening
The old castle was dark and **spooky**.

spot (n)

speck, stain, smudge, blot
There is a **spot** of dirt on your jumper.

spot (v)

1. see, notice, observe, catch sight of
I didn't **spot** the tiger before it jumped out.

2. identify, find
Can you **spot** the five differences?

spread (v)

1. circulate, pass
The news **spread** quickly around the town.

2. lay out, distribute, arrange
Let's **spread** out the pictures on the table to look at them.

3. smear
Beatrice **spread** butter on her bread.

4. extend, stretch, expand
The tea will **spread** across the tablecloth if it's not mopped up.
opposite: *contract*

spring (v)

bound, leap, jump, bounce
A young lamb can **spring** around a field soon after birth.

squash (v)

squeeze, press, compress, crush, mash
We had to **squash** the clothes into the suitcase.

squeeze (v)

1. squash, press, cram, wedge, stuff
We had to **squeeze** into our tiny car.

2. wring, press
Squeeze all the water from your
costume after you've been swimming.

stack (n)

pile, tower, column, heap
My dad keeps a **stack** of wood
in the shed.

stamp (v)

1. trample, tread, tramp
The explorers **stamp** across the
snowy fields.

2. mark
They will **stamp** your passport
before you get on the plane.

stand (v)

1. be upright, be vertical, stand up
My grandma finds it difficult to
stand for a long time.

2. stand up, rise, be upstanding
Please **stand** so I can count you.

3. bear, endure, put up with, tolerate
Anya can't **stand** rice pudding.

4. place, position, set
Stand the suitcase over there.

5. support, defend, speak up for
A friend will **stand up for** you in
an argument.

standard (adj)

normal, average, medium, regular
This hat is a **standard** size.

start (n)

opening, introduction, launch,
beginning, commencement
Our team will perform at the **start**
of the gala.
opposite: *finish*

start (v)

1. begin, commence, get going
Our holiday will **start** on Friday.
opposite: *finish, end*

2. set up, create, launch, open,
introduce
The school is going to **start** a drama
club on Tuesdays.

stay (v)

1. remain, wait, linger, hang around
Dad will **stay** at home with me while
mum goes to fetch my cousin.

2. keep, remain
Use your seatbelt to **stay** safe in
the car.

3. visit, live in, spend time at,
remain at
We will **stay at** my aunt's house for
the weekend.

steady (adj)

1. unwavering, firm, stable
The painter has a **steady** hand.
opposite: *shaky*

2. even, regular, smooth
The horses kept up a **steady** pace round the racetrack.
opposite: *varied*

3. continuous, unbroken, constant
There was a **steady** stream of water from the broken pipe.
opposite: *intermittent*

step (v)

tread, stamp, walk, trample
Mind you don't **step** on the glass!

stick (n)

branch, twig, bough
We collected **sticks** to make into fishing rods.

stick (v)

1. join, fix, glue, bond, fasten
Stick the two halves together.
opposite: *separate*

2. poke, jab, thrust
Don't **stick** your elbow into me – it hurts!

stick out (v)

protrude, poke out
It is rude to **stick out** your tongue.

stick up (v)

support, defend, speak up for, side with
I will **stick up for** you if you're in trouble.
opposite: *denounce*

stiff (adj)

1. painful, tense, aching, sore
My muscles are **stiff** after going running.
opposite: *loose*

2. firm, solid, unbending, hard
Rachel drew a picture and stuck it on to **stiff** card.
opposite: *flexible*

a
b
c
d
e
f
g
h
i
j
k
l
m
n
o
p
q
r
s
t
u
v
w
x
y
z

still (adj)

1. stationary, unmoving, motionless, immobile
The antelope kept **still** when it saw the lion.

2. calm, peaceful, quiet, tranquil
The sea is **still** this afternoon.

stir (v)

1. mix, agitate, blend
The witch told the boy to **stir** the potion in the cauldron.

2. move, shift
Restless people **stir** in their sleep.

stone (n)

rock, boulder, pebble
I tripped over a **stone** on the path.

stop (v)

1. halt, draw up, pull up
Stop when you get to the lights.
opposite: *keep going*

2. prevent, block
Mum will **stop** me going out in the dark.

3. give up, abandon, quit
Uncle John must **stop** drinking tea.
opposite: *continue*

4. finish, end
The archery course will **stop** if there aren't enough participants.

store (v)

1. keep, stash, stow
We **store** our vegetables in a basket in the kitchen.

2. stockpile, hoard
My neighbour likes to **store** cans of food in case there is an emergency.

a b c d e f g h i j k l m n o p q r **s** t u v w x y z

a
b
c
d
e
f
g
h
i
j
k
l
m
n
o
p
q
r
s
t
u
v
w
x
y
z

strange (adj)

1. odd, weird, bizarre, peculiar, unusual, remarkable, funny
The boy next door plays **strange** music.
opposite: *ordinary*

2. bewildering, puzzling, mysterious
The children heard **strange** noises coming from the cellar.
opposite: *normal*

3. unfamiliar, new, unknown
I don't like to stay in **strange** places.
opposite: *familiar*

strength (n)

power, might, force
I don't have the **strength** to fight another dragon.
opposite: *weakness*

strong (adj)

1. powerful, mighty, robust
Jessica was **strong** enough to battle the giant unaided.
opposite: *weak*

2. concentrated, potent
The boss made a **strong** cup of tea for each of the workers.
opposite: *dilute*

3. sturdy, robust, tough, substantial
The builders used a **strong** cart to carry all the rocks.
opposite: *flimsy*

stuff (n)

1. possessions, goods, things, belongings
We put all our **stuff** into storage and sailed round the world.

2. matter, substance, material
There's some orange **stuff** stuck to my shirt.

stuff (v)

pack, force, push, squeeze, squash, cram, crowd
Dad tried to **stuff** all our clothes into one bag.

stupid (adj)

1. ignorant, dumb, dense, slow, thick
The giant was rather **stupid**, but the little girl helped him with his lessons.
opposite: *clever*

2. foolish, unwise, silly, idiotic, crazy, nuts
It's **stupid** to lean out of the window in a moving train.
opposite: *smart*

3. senseless, nonsensical, absurd, daft
My little brother told a **stupid** story about a goat with a blue hat.

sure (adj)

certain, positive, confident
Are you **sure** you fed the guinea pig?
opposite: *uncertain*

surprise (n)

1. astonishment, wonder, amazement
Sophia gasped in **surprise** when she saw the present.

2. bombshell, shock
It was certainly a **surprise** to discover Patrick was really an alien.

surprise (v)

1. astonish, thrill, amaze, astound, stagger, take aback
Maddie was **surprised** by the news that she had won the contest.

2. startle, catch unawares
Let's **surprise** Mum by jumping out from behind the sofa.

swap (v)

exchange, trade, switch, change
Would you **swap** two satsumas for your banana?

swing (v)

hang, sway, dangle
Micha liked to **swing** by his legs on the climbing frame.

switch (v)

1. turn
Don't forget to **switch** off the lights when you leave the room.

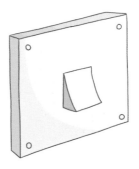

2. swap, exchange
Tim wants to **switch** his bad drawing for Anton's good one.

a
b
c
d
e
f
g
h
i
j
k
l
m
n
o
p
q
r
s
t
u
v
w
x
y
z

a
b
c
d
e
f
g
h
i
j
k
l
m
n
o
p
q
r
s
t
u
v
w
x
y
z

Tt

take (v)
See page 128

talk (n)
1. lecture, presentation, report
Hassan gave a **talk** about sharks to the class.

2. chat (with), discussion (with), conversation (with)
Sarah's mother had a **talk** to her about her bad behaviour.

talk (v)
chat, speak, gossip, chatter, converse, natter
Please don't **talk** during lessons.

tall (adj)
high, large, towering, soaring
We gazed up at the **tall** building.
opposite: *short, small*

tap (v)
touch, rap, poke
Barney **tapped** Talia on the shoulder.

taste (n)
1. flavour
I hate the **taste** of tomatoes.

2. bite, morsel, mouthful, nibble
Please can I have a **taste** of your ice cream?
See also page 124

teach (v)
show, instruct, educate, coach
If you want to play an instrument, the musician will **teach** you.

tear (n)
rip, gash, rent, slit, split, hole
There is a **tear** in the flag.

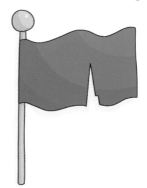

tear (v)
1. rip, split, snag
If you fall, you will **tear** your fancy-dress costume.

2. dash, rush, run, hurry, hurtle, race, speed
We saw the dog **tear** down the street after a cat.

tease (v)

taunt, make fun of, jeer at, ridicule, mock, laugh at
It's cruel to **tease** people.

tell (v)

1. inform, notify, let know
Please **tell** Benjamin that it's time to come inside now.

2. narrate, relate, recite
I will **tell** you a story if you like.

3. command, order, instruct, demand that
If I **tell** you to do something, I expect you to do it.

4. reveal, disclose, explain, describe
Tell me what you have discovered.

5. know, decide, determine, work out, calculate
We can't **tell** whether the floodwater will reach the shops.

terrible (adj)

awful, horrible, horrid, monstrous, diabolical, dreadful, appalling, shocking, frightful, horrendous
The **terrible** monster ate Bernard.

terrific (adj)

wonderful, great, amazing, brilliant, marvellous, outstanding, stunning, first-rate, top-notch, exceptional
We had a **terrific** time at the zoo.

terror (n)

fright, horror, fear, dread, panic
Thomas ran off in **terror** when he saw the wolf.

test (n)

1. exam, examination, quiz, assessment
The teacher gave the children a surprise spelling **test**.

2. check
The car had to go to the garage for a **test**.

thick (adj)

1. dense, heavy
There is a **thick** fog over the bay.

2. wide, broad
This piece of wood is too **thick** to cut.
opposite: *thin*

3. sturdy, stout, heavy, solid, strong
There is a **thick** barrier along the cliff edge.

4. stupid, dense, idiotic, dumb
They thought I was being **thick** because I didn't know how to do it.

thief (n)
burglar, robber, mugger,
pickpocket, shoplifter
The **thief** stole a sackful of treasure.

thin (adj)
1. slim, slender, narrow, skinny,
slight, scrawny
The new fawn has very **thin** legs.
opposite: *fat*

2. light, flimsy, delicate, fine, sheer
The fortune-teller wore a veil of
thin fabric.
opposite: *thick*

thing (n)
item, object, article
There is one **thing** left in the suitcase.

things (n)
stuff, gear, kit, equipment,
bits and pieces
I can't go swimming because I've left
all my **things** at home.

think (v)
1. suppose, guess, expect, believe
Do you **think** it will snow this winter?

2. concentrate
I have to **think** hard to work out the
answers to these questions.

thought (n)
idea, brainwave
I had a **thought** as I got out of
the bath.

thrilled (adj)
delighted, overjoyed, ecstatic,
bowled over
Barney was **thrilled** with his
new scooter.

throw (v)
1. toss, fling, chuck, hurl
Would you like to **throw** a stick
to the dog?

2. chuck out, discard, get rid of,
dump, dispose of
We need to **throw away** this rubbish.

a
b
c
d
e
f
g
h
i
j
k
l
m
n
o
p
q
r
s
t
u
v
w
x
y
z

tidy (adj)

neat, arranged, uncluttered, orderly
Your room is **tidy** for once!
opposite: *messy*

tie (v)

1. knot, fasten, do up
Tie your laces and we will go outside.

2. secure, bind, loop, fix, attach
The cook will **tie** a ribbon round
the cake.

tight (adj)

secure, firm, fixed, fast
The knot is too **tight** to undo.
opposite: *loose*

2. restricted, narrow, cramped,
crowded
The audience was squeezed into a
tight space.
opposite: *open*

time (n)

1. occasion, moment, opportunity
This is a good **time** to think about
getting a pet.

2. promptly, punctually
Will we get there on **time**?

3. a period, a while
We will spend **some time** with our
friends in Italy.

tiny (adj)

small, minute, miniscule, mini, little
There is a **tiny** mouse in the shed.
opposite: *large*, *big*

tip (n)

1. point, end, top
The **tip** of the pencil was blunt.
opposite: *base*

2. dump
Dad took the rubbish to the **tip**.

3. advice, hint, clue, suggestion
Clive gave me a good **tip** on how
to fly my kite.

tired (adj)

weary, exhausted, sleepy, worn out
After playing on the beach all day,
Amelia was **tired**.

top (n)

1. lid, cover, cap
Put the **top** on when you have
finished with the jam.

2. peak, summit, tip, crest
The boys climbed to the **top** of
the hill.

a
b
c
d
e
f
g
h
i
j
k
l
m
n
o
p
q
r
s
t
u
v
w
x
y
z

top (adj)

1. highest, uppermost
The bird's nest is on the **top** branch.
opposite: *lowest*

2. best, highest
I got the **top** score in the quiz.
opposite: *bottom*

3. leading, fine, excellent, foremost
Our music teacher is a **top** violinist.

total (adj)

1. utter, absolute, complete, downright
The school play was a **total** disaster.

2. whole, entire
The **total** number of people entering
the competition was fifty-six.

totally

entirely, absolutely, wholly, completely
Robbie was **totally** exhausted after
his long run.

touch (v)

stroke, pat, rub, fondle, handle, feel
Make sure you **touch** the rabbit
gently so you don't scare her.

touched (adj)

moved, affected
Becky was **touched** by the large
number of cards she received
in hospital.
opposite: *unmoved*

track (n)

1. path, pathway, footpath, trail
We followed the narrow **track**
through the fields.

2. footprints, trace, spoor, trail
Rory found badger **tracks** in
the snow.

3. line, rails
The train raced down the **track**.

track (v)

1. follow, trace, trail, pursue,
tail, stalk
The children can **track** the pirates to
their island hideaway.
opposite: *lost*

2. find, discover, identify
It's the policeman's job to **track down**
the thief.

trap (v)

catch, snare, capture
The farmer set out to **trap** the wolf
that had attacked his sheep.

tremble (v)

shake, shiver, quiver, quake
The mouse will **tremble** if it sees
a cat.

trick (v)

fool, dupe, deceive, cheat
Peter's brother **tricked** him into getting up an hour too early.

tricky (adj)

difficult, awkward, hard, complicated
We tackled some **tricky** climbs on our last expedition.
opposite: *easy*

trip (n)

voyage, journey, expedition, safari, outing
The family went on a **trip** to Kenya.

trip (v)

fall, stumble, slip, lose one's footing
People will **trip** if you leave your toys in the way.

trouble (n)

1. commotion, bother, disorder, disturbance
There was a lot of **trouble** in the playground.
2. problem, difficulty
The **trouble** with the car prevented us from going away.
3. bother, effort
Dad went to a lot of **trouble** to get tickets for the show.

trouble (v)

bother, interrupt, hassle, disturb
We are not allowed to **trouble** Mum while she is working.

true (adj)

1. accurate, honest, truthful, factual
The amazing story Uncle Jack told us was **true**.
opposite: *untrue*
2. faithful, genuine, authentic, real, loyal
Sebastian was a **true** friend who stood by us in difficult times.
opposite: *false*

try (n)

attempt, go, effort
Elsie had a really good **try**, but she could not beat the record.

try (v)

1. attempt, endeavour, struggle, strive
We will **try** to get to the event on time.
2. sample, test
Would you like to **try** the new cherry ice cream?

turn

turn (n)

1. chance, go, opportunity
It is nearly my **turn** to go on the swings.

2. trip, circuit
We took a **turn** round the park.

turn (v)

1. twirl, whirl, spin, revolve
The dancer can **turn** round and round really quickly.

2. rotate, twist
You have to **turn** the handle all the way round.

3. swerve, curve, bank, veer
The aeroplane **turned** suddenly to the left.

4. swivel, rotate, swing, spin, roll, revolve
The top of the toy robot **turns** on a ball bearing.

5. transform, change
Witches **turn** princes into frogs.

6. convert, develop
Let's **turn** our driveway into a garden.

twist (v)

1. coil, loop, wind, curl
Let the snake **twist** round your arm.

2. curve, weave, zigzag, meander
The paths **twist** through the forest.

3. turn, rotate
Twist the lid to open the jar.

two

a couple of, a pair of
There are **two** birds on the branch.

type (n)

sort, kind, brand, variety
Which **type** of sausage would you like?

Uu

ugly (adj)

unattractive, plain, hideous, repulsive
The **ugly** witch lived in a filthy hovel.
opposite: *beautiful*

uncertain (adj)

unsure, doubtful
I was **uncertain** what to say to my
great aunt.

uncomfortable (adj)

1. hard, stiff, lumpy, rough
The new chair we bought is
uncomfortable.
opposite: *comfortable*
2. uneasy, embarrassed, awkward
Poppy felt **uncomfortable** singing
in front of all the parents.
opposite: *confident*

under

beneath, below, underneath
There is a troll **under** that bridge.
opposite: *above*

uneven (adj)

bumpy, lumpy, rough
The surface of the road was **uneven**.
opposite: *level*

unfair (adj)

unjust, wrong, unreasonable
It was **unfair** that Anton had three
turns on the roundabout and I had
only one.
opposite: *fair*

unfriendly (adj)

1. hostile, antagonistic, fierce
The **unfriendly** dog snarled as Jamie
walked past.
opposite: *friendly*
2. aloof, unapproachable,
stuck-up, snobbish
The new family down the road
is very **unfriendly**.
opposite: *welcoming*

unhappy (adj)

sad, miserable, upset, depressed,
mournful, gloomy, disappointed,
distressed
Ryan was **unhappy** when his
hamster died.
opposite: *happy*

a
b
c
d
e
f
g
h
i
j
k
l
m
n
o
p
q
r
s
t
u
v
w
x
y
z

unkind (adj)

mean, cruel, vicious, spiteful, nasty, stern, harsh
The wizard was **unkind** to his helpers.
opposite: *kind*

unusual (adj)

strange, funny, odd, rare, scarce, unfamiliar, exceptional, extraordinary
We saw an **unusual** type of fish in the river.
opposite: *ordinary*

upset (v)

1. annoy, irritate, aggravate, distress
Try not to **upset** your mother on her birthday.
2. spilt, tipped over, knocked over, overturned
Jake **upset** the milk over the table.

upset (adj)

1. unhappy, miserable, distressed, distraught, alarmed, worried, sad
Stan was very **upset** when he heard his granny was ill.
opposite: *happy*
2. disappointed, irritated, annoyed
Mum was **upset** that the car had broken down again.
opposite: *content, pleased*

urgent (adj)

important, pressing, top-priority
This letter is **urgent**. Please post it immediately.

use (n)

good, point, benefit
What **use** is this broken kettle?

use (v)

1. work, employ, operate, run
Does anyone know how to **use** the photocopier?
2. consume, expend
We **use** too much paper.

useless (adj)

1. worthless, no good
This broken laptop is **useless**.
opposite: *useful*
2. bad, incompetent, rubbish, no good
I am **useless** at playing the piano.
opposite: *skilled*

usually

generally, normally, as a rule, most of the time, in general, mostly
I **usually** beat my sister at chess.

Vv

valuable (adj)

1. precious, costly, expensive
The necklace that the thief took
was **valuable**.
opposite: *worthless*

2. useful, worthwhile, invaluable,
good, constructive
The nurse gave us **valuable** advice
about looking after ourselves.
opposite: *useless*

value (n)

1. worth, cost, price
This sports equipment has a
high **value**.

2. benefit, advantage, use, usefulness
The lifeguard explained the **value** of
learning to swim.

value (v)

1. prize, appreciate, esteem, respect
We **value** the caretaker's help in
cleaning up the mess.
opposite: *disregard*

2. evaluate, estimate, appraise
The estate agent is coming to **value**
our house.

very

See page 128

view (n)

1. outlook, vista, scene, panorama
There is a good **view** from the top of
the hill.

2. opinion, mind
In my **view**, school dinners should
always be hot.

visit (v)

1. go to, see, stay in
We will **visit** Berlin in the spring.

2. call on, drop round on
I'm going to **visit** my friend.

visitor (n)

guest, caller
We had a **visitor** for supper
last week.

a
b
c
d
e
f
g
h
i
j
k
l
m
n
o
p
q
r
s
t
u
v
w
x
y
z

Ww

wait (v)

1. hang on, stop, hang around
We had to **wait** ages for lunch.

2. remain, linger, pause
Wait here while I pop into this shop.

wake (v)

1. get up, rise, stir, wake up
I usually **wake** at 7 o'clock in the morning.
opposite: *go to sleep*

2. rouse, awaken
Mum will **wake** me early tomorrow as there is a school trip.

walk (n)

stroll, hike, trek, saunter, wander
We went for a **walk** as it was a sunny day.

walk (v)

1. tread, pace, step, stride
Do not **walk** on the grass.

2. pad, patter
The dog **walks** slowly across the kitchen floor.

3. trudge, march, troop, trek, stride
The soldiers **walk** for miles across the windy desert.

4. crawl, creep, inch
A spider **walked** over my arm.

5. hobble, stagger, lurch, shuffle, limp, stumble
The injured man managed to **walk** to the side of the road.

want (v)

desire, long for, wish for, would like
I **want** a new computer game for my birthday.

war (n)

conflict, fight, battle
The **war** between the two countries has lasted for ten years.

warm (adj)

1. mild, temperate, slightly hot
It is a **warm** and sunny day.
opposite: *cool*

2. tepid, lukewarm
I like to drink **warm** milk.

wash (n)
bath, shower
Have a good **wash** before bed.

wash (v)
clean, cleanse, launder, rinse, scrub, sponge down
I need to **wash** my face after eating chocolate ice cream.

watch (v)
1. observe, gaze at, view
Matilda is going to **watch** the ships on the sea.

2. see
Did you **watch** that film last night?

3. look after, guard, mind, attend to, keep an eye on
Please **watch** the baby while I answer the phone.

wave (n)
1. swell, ripple, breaker, surf
We played in the **waves** at the edge of the sea.

2. surge, episode, outbreak, epidemic
A second **wave** of illness swept through the school.

wave (v)
1. move to and fro, flap, flutter, swing
The flag **waved** in the breeze.

2. shake, waggle, brandish
The angry man in the park **waved** his stick at us.

way (n)
1. route, directions, path
Do you know the **way** to the forest?

2. method, technique, process
What is the right **way** way to make a cake?

3. regard
In one **way**, my sister is just like me.

weak (adj)
1. feeble, puny, powerless
The boy was too **weak** to lift the weight.
opposite: *strong*

2. faint, small, indistinct, dim
The light from the lamp was **weak**.
opposite: *bright*

a b c d e f g h i j k l m n o p q r s t u v **w** x y z

well

1. ably, brilliantly, competently, thoroughly, admirably, efficiently, effectively
You managed that task really **well**!

2. closely, intimately
I know that dog **well** – he won't hurt us.

wet (adj)

1. damp, soaked, drenched, saturated, dripping, sopping
I am **wet** because I was caught in the rain.

2. soggy, waterlogged, sodden
The ground is too **wet** for us to play football.

3. rainy, drizzling, pouring
It has been **wet** all afternoon.

while (n)

time, moment, interval, period
After a **while**, the tiger stopped growling.

whole (adj)

1. entire, complete, all of
Mohammed ate the **whole** loaf of bread.

2. complete, unbroken, intact
Take a photo of the birthday cake while it's still **whole**.

wicked (adj)

evil, cruel, nasty, sinful
The **wicked** queen tried to kill Snow White.

wide (adj)

broad, large, vast, expansive
The pioneers crossed the **wide** plain, heading for the mountains.
opposite: *narrow*

wild (adj)

1. natural, uncultivated
The children collected **wild** berries.
opposite: *cultivated*

2. untamed, undomesticated
I like to draw **wild** animals.
opposite: *tame*

3. berserk, crazy, demented
The lion went **wild**, and roared all night.
opposite: *calm*

118

win (n)

victory, triumph, success, conquest
We celebrated our **win** with a trip to
a café.
opposite: *loss*

win (v)

1. come first, triumph, be victorious,
prevail, succeed
Do you think we will **win**?
opposite: *lose*

2. achieve, gain, take, secure
I knew Stevie would **win** first prize in
the swimming gala.
opposite: *miss*

wind (v)

1. coil, twist, turn, loop
Wind the wool round your hands.

2. weave, twist, curve, meander
The river **winds** through
the mountains.

windy (adj)

blustery, stormy, breezy, gusty
It was a **windy** day, so we went
to fly our kites.

wish (n)

1. longing, desire, craving, dream
Scarlett's dearest **wish** was for a
kitten of her own.

2. favour, request, demand
The genie will grant you three **wishes**.

wish (v)

long, desire, would love, yearn, crave
I **wish** to become an astronaut.

wonderful (adj)

amazing, brilliant, outstanding,
sensational, terrific, excellent,
awesome
We saw a **wonderful** painting
at the museum.

wood (n)

1. forest, grove, woodland, copse,
orchard, jungle
The two children dropped a trail
of breadcrumbs as they wandered
into the **wood**.

2. timber
My grandma has a coffee table
made of polished **wood**.

a
b
c
d
e
f
g
h
i
j
k
l
m
n
o
p
q
r
s
t
u
v
w
x
y
z

a
b
c
d
e
f
g
h
i
j
k
l
m
n
o
p
q
r
s
t
u
v
w
x
y
z

work (n)

1. job, career, profession, occupation, employment
What type of **work** would you like to do when you grow up?

2. preparation, study
I have done lots of **work** for my music test.

3. task, assignment, project, homework
Have you finished your **work** on pond animals?

work (v)

toil at, labour at, persevere with, practise
You will have to **work at** your tennis if you want to be in the school team.

world (n)

Earth, globe, planet
There are no more dodos anywhere in the **world**.

worried (adj)

anxious, nervous, afraid (of), concerned, perturbed
Neil is **worried** about going to hospital next week.

wound (n)

sore, injury, gash, cut, graze
Rita has a nasty **wound** on her leg.

wriggle (v)

squirm, writhe, wiggle
The worm **wriggled** slowly along the ground.

write (v)

print, sign, scrawl, inscribe
Please **write** your name at the top of the paper.

writer (n)

author, journalist, poet, storyteller
She wants to be a **writer** when she grows up.

wrong (adj)

incorrect, inaccurate, erroneous
I think I gave the **wrong** answer to the last question.
opposite: *right, correct*

Y y

yell (v)

shout, call, cry out, bellow, scream
If you **yell** loudly enough, they will
hear you at the end of the street.

young (adj)

juvenile, immature, newborn, infant,
youthful
A **young** seal can swim immediately
after birth.
opposite: *old*

Z z

zero (n)

nought, nothing, nil, zilch
My uncle's car can go from **zero**
to eighty miles per hour in
seven seconds.

Topic words

These lists will help you to find new words to use in your writing.

Adventures

dangerous, dramatic, electrifying, exciting, exhausting, fascinating, frightening, fun, hair-raising, incredible, intriguing, mysterious, nail-biting, nerve-wracking, puzzling, scary, sinister, tense, terrifying, thrilling

Animals

beastly, bristly, feathery, fluffy, friendly, furry, hairy, scaly, scary, shaggy, silky, sleek, smooth, soft, spiky, tame, wild, woolly

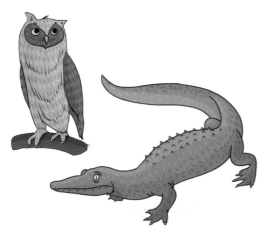

Buildings

ancient, crumbling, futuristic, historic, imposing, magnificent, modern, old, refurbished, ruined, striking, towering

Clothes

baggy, casual, chic, comfortable, cool, cropped, fashionable, fitted, flattering, hooded, light, long, loose, scruffy, short, smart, sporty, stretchy, tight, warm

Colours

black: ebony, sable

blue: azure, cobalt, kingfisher, sea blue, sky blue

brown: beige, brass, bronze, chocolate, fawn, tan, tawny

green: emerald, jade, leaf green, turquoise

grey: charcoal, dove grey, silver

orange: ginger, ochre, peach

pink: cerise, rose

purple: lilac, mauve

red: blood red, crimson, magenta, maroon, ruby, scarlet

yellow: amber, apricot, blonde (hair), gold, golden, honey-coloured

white: cream, ivory, pearl

Cooking

bake, barbecue, beat, blanch, boil, chop, freeze, fry, grill, melt, microwave, mix, peel, poach, prepare, refrigerate, roast, simmer, sizzle, steam, stew, stir, toast

Feelings

afraid, amused, angry, anxious, astonished, bored, calm, cheerful, confident, cross, depressed, disappointed, embarrassed, enthusiastic, envious, excited, frightened, frustrated, gloomy, grateful, grouchy, grumpy, happy, homesick, in love, insecure, jealous, lonely, miserable, nervous, pleased, proud, relieved, sad, scared, shy, sleepy, tense, thoughtful, tired, upset, worried

Groups

clutch of eggs
flock of birds, sheep
herd of cows, goats
litter of kittens, puppies
nest of snakes
pack of wolves, dogs
pod of whales
pride of lions
school of dolphins
shoal of fish
swarm of bees

Human body

athletic, bent, bony, crooked, fat, hairy, heavy, lanky, muscular, petite, plump, short, skinny, smooth, stocky, stooped, stout, strong, tall, thin, weak, wrinkled, youthful

Materials

blunt, bright, bumpy, dull, heavy, light, rough, scratchy, sharp, shiny, smooth

Movement

climb, cycle, dive, fall, fly, gallop, haul, hop, hurl, hurtle, jump, leap, pull, push, ride, rise, run, soar, shove, skip, sprint, swim, throw, trot, tumble

Music

bouncy, catchy, fast, jaunty, jazzy, lively, repetitive, rhythmic, rousing, slow, stirring, tuneful

Taste

bitter, bland, delicious, disgusting, fruity, mild, savoury, spicy, sweet, tangy, yummy

Weather

cloudy: gloomy, grey, overcast

cold: bitter, chilly, freezing, frosty, icy, nippy, snowy

fine: balmy, bright, calm, clear, dry, mild, sunny, warm

foggy: hazy, misty, murky

hot: baking, boiling, roasting, scorching, sweltering

humid: close, muggy, oppressive, thundery, steamy, sticky

rainy: damp, drizzly, pouring, showery, spitting, tipping down, torrential, wet

windy: blowy, blustery, breezy, stormy

Overused words

Some words have quite a broad meaning. Your writing will be more interesting if you can think of a more exact or specific word. Here are some examples to help you.

bad

I had a **bad** day.
difficult, disappointing, frustrating, miserable, tiring, trying, unpleasant

I have a **bad** headache.
nasty, painful, serious, severe, stabbing, throbbing

The meal was **bad**.
disgusting, tasteless, vile

The fish has gone **bad**.
mouldy, off, rancid, rotten

You have been **bad**.
cruel, disobedient, inconsiderate, mean, mischievous, naughty, thoughtless, unkind

She got a **bad** result in the test.
below average, disappointing, low, poor, substandard, unworthy

get

How did you **get** that skateboard?
acquire, come by, obtain

We can **get** food from the kitchen.
bring, carry, fetch

I **got** sick after eating old sausages.
become, fall, feel

He **gets** pocket money each week.
be given, earn, have, receive

She **gets** tired at the end of the day.
become, feel, grow

We need to **get away from** here.
depart, leave

The prisoner will **get away**.
escape, slip off

We need to **get going** before dark.
begin, depart, leave, set off, start

Get in the vehicle.
board, climb aboard, embark

We can **get off** at the next stop.
disembark, dismount

He doesn't **get on with** his step-sister.
feel at ease with, like, see eye to eye

How is she **getting on** at school?
coping, doing, fitting in, making progress, progressing

Will she **get over** the shock?
recover from, survive

We need to **get rid of** the rubbish.
dispose of, lose, throw away

The farmer must **get rid of** the slugs.
destroy, kill, wipe out

How can we **get through** this ordeal?
endure, live through, survive

He can **get through** the jungle with that large knife.
hack through, penetrate

What time did you **get up**?
appear, awaken, jump out of bed, rise, rise and shine

go

We will **go** to town.
cycle, drive, jog, run, saunter, sprint, stroll, take the bus/train, tramp, travel, trudge, walk

The balloon will **go up** in the air.
ascend, drift up, float, rise

The boat will **go** over the sea.
cross, drift, float, paddle, power, sail, steam

Shall we **go** in here?
call, crawl, creep, dodge, drop, enter, pop, run, sneak

have

I **have** four cats.
care for, keep, look after, own, possess

We will **have** a party next week.
hold, host, organize, put on, stage, throw

Will you **have** another cake?
choose, eat, take

We might **have** trouble finding your house.
experience, face, meet with, run into

I **have** a cold.
be ill with, catch, develop, suffer from

The book **has** free stickers.
be accompanied by, come with, include

Jo **had** lots of birthday cards.
be given, be sent, receive

My dog **had** puppies.
bear, give birth to, produce

lovely

I have a **lovely** new T-shirt.
bright, brilliant, colourful, cool, great, handsome, jazzy, pretty, snug, trendy, warm, well-made

It is a **lovely** day.
beautiful, fine, glorious, gorgeous ideal, mild, perfect, pleasant, spectacular, sunny, sweltering, warm

We had a **lovely** dinner.
delicious, friendly, gorgeous, relaxed, scrumptious, tasty, yummy

Hannah has a **lovely** kitten.
adorable, bouncy, cute, endearing fluffy, friendly, playful

We had a **lovely** time at the beach.
awesome, brilliant, delightful, enjoyable, fabulous, fantastic, great, pleasant, pleasing, wonderful

My cousin is **lovely**.
charming, delightful, enchanting likeable, lovable, sweet

move

I can't **move** an inch.
budge, crawl, creep, shift, shuffle, stagger, walk

Move quickly! A lion is coming!
bound, dash, hurry, hurtle, leap, race, run, rush, speed, sprint, zoom

We must **move** from here.
depart, flee, go, leave, quit, run away

The bear will **move back** if you raise your stick.
back away, retreat, reverse, withdraw

We will **move up** the hill soon.
ascend, climb up, mount, rise up

Please **move** towards the gate.
advance, approach, go, proceed, progress

nice (*see also* lovely)

She has a **nice** new friend.
amiable, bouncy, clever, easy-going, energetic, friendly, funny, good-natured, imaginative, lively, sweet, sympathetic, talented, warm-hearted

That lesson on pond life was **nice**.
amusing, captivating, entertaining, fun, interesting

Apples taste **nice**.
delicious, enjoyable, scrumptious, sweet, yummy

put

Put the letters in the box.
chuck, conceal, deposit, hide, place, position, store, throw, toss

Put on a brave face.
adopt, assume, fake

Put your name at the top of the page.
fill in, insert, type, write

Please **put away** your toys.
pack away, pick up, store, stow, tidy

say

"What did you do?" **says** Abbie.
ask, complain, demand, gasp,
giggle, groan, grumble, inquire, laugh,
query, question, sigh, smile, sob, wail,
whine, whinge

"It's a boy!" the doctor **says**.
announce, declare, exclaim, state

Sam will **say** it wasn't his fault.
assert, claim, insist, profess, promise

What do you **say**?
reckon, suggest, think

"Hooray!" we all **say**.
cheer, chorus, cry, exclaim,
scream, shout

Some people **say** it was Chris who stole
the dinner money.
allege, assert, claim, report, suggest

Say your lines out loud.
deliver, perform, read, recite, rehearse

Only Dad has any **say** in this decision.
influence, input, sway, voice, vote

take

I must **take** these books to school.
carry, transport

Thieves **take** other
people's things.
carry away, nick,
pinch, snatch, steal

We will **take** a trip to the coast.
embark on, go on, make, organize,
set out on

We will **take** four boxes of cakes.
buy, order, purchase, receive

I will **take** the shoes back to the shop.
return

You must **take** your medicine.
consume, drink, eat, swallow

She wanted to **take** a train to Paris.
book, catch, go on, join

very

It is **very** scary in here.
astonishingly, extraordinarily,
extremely, unusually

*Look at the word you are using 'very'
with; can you find a better word for
both of them together?*

very hot: baking, boiling, fiery,
scalding, scorching

very angry: enraged, fuming,
furious, livid

very hungry: ravenous, starving

Ladybird I'm Ready...
to Spell!

Thesaurus

Written by Anne Rooney
Illustrated by Tom Heard

LADYBIRD BOOKS

UK | USA | Canada | Ireland | Australia
India | New Zealand | South Africa

Ladybird Books is part of the Penguin Random House group of companies
whose addresses can be found at global.penguinrandomhouse.com

ladybird.com

First published 2015

001

Copyright © Ladybird Books Ltd, 2015

Ladybird and the Ladybird logo are registered trademarks owned by Ladybird Books Ltd

The moral right of the author and illustrator has been asserted

Printed in China

A CIP catalogue record for this book is available from the British Library

ISBN: 978–0–723–29550–1